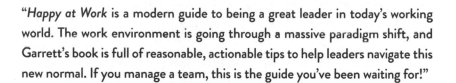

"*Happy at Work* is a modern guide to being a great leader in today's working world. The work environment is going through a massive paradigm shift, and Garrett's book is full of reasonable, actionable tips to help leaders navigate this new normal. If you manage a team, this is the guide you've been waiting for!"

—Colin Rocker, TikTok career influencer

"*Happy at Work* is a clarion call for modern executives to stop talking about culture and start building it with passion and intention. Robyn L. Garrett highlights the economic benefits of being happy at work and offers a practical path forward that's accessible to anyone with the courage to take the first step."

—Gregory Offner Jr., author of *Tip Jar Culture*

"My favorite is Chapter 7, which is all about how to achieve work-life balance. My daily battle! I got great *tactical* advice, with examples laid out nicely for me. Garrett's tone made me feel ready and accepted. On the go? Each chapter lays out what to expect, and you won't be disappointed. She gets right to the point and makes me feel confident about facing my challenges head-on. Don't walk to get this book—*run!*"

—Elainy Mata, *Harvard Business Review*

"What I particularly love about Garrett's premise is that we are all accountable for our own happiness. As leaders, it's our job to role-model this accountability and create a culture that allows our team the space to create their own happiness. I love that Garrett is creating this 'how-to' book that today's—and tomorrow's—leaders can use to reshape the corporate environment."

—Mel Savage, executive coach, host of *The Career Reset* podcast

PRAISE FOR *HAPPY AT WORK*

"Creating a thriving workplace culture is crucial in today's rapidly changing workplace. Robyn L. Garrett's groundbreaking book, *Happy at Work*, gives you one hundred strategies to transform your work environment into a supportive, flexible, productive, and happy one. It's an essential read for leaders who want to cultivate a culture in which employees feel valued and motivated. *Happy at Work* isn't just a collection of ideas; it's a road map to a better workplace, and it deserves to be on the reading list of every leader who wants to create a productive, successful, and welcoming workplace."

—Jhánee Carter, founder and CEO of The HRQUEEN

"*Happy at Work* is a practical and timely guide to help organizations be competitive in the talent market and, more importantly, build a workplace that people want to spend their time and energy supporting. The world of work has changed dramatically since the pandemic—the old ways of work are simply and unnecessarily destroying the human spirit. Leaders need a new guide, and Garrett has brilliantly outlined it for them."

—Kara Kirby, host of *Pop! On Leadership* podcast

"There are very few books on leadership and career development that I'd strongly recommend because the approaches are old-school, academic, fear-based models. Garrett's approach—especially with the focus of engagement, satisfaction, happiness, and self-discovery—is one of the few that was delightful to read. As a human resources business partner who has had meaningful career discussions with people from their first internship to retiring CMOs, employees of all ages and disciplines would find a great deal of value from this."

—Daniel Space, a.k.a. Dan from HR on LinkedIn, TikTok, and Twitter

happy @ WORK

How to Create a
Happy, Engaging
Workplace
for Today's (and Tomorrow's!) Workforce

Robyn L. Garrett

ADAMS MEDIA

NEW YORK   LONDON   TORONTO   SYDNEY   NEW DELHI

Adams Media
An Imprint of Simon & Schuster, Inc.
100 Technology Center Drive
Stoughton, Massachusetts 02072

First Adams Media trade paperback edition September 2023

ADAMS MEDIA and colophon are registered trademarks of Simon & Schuster, Inc.

For information about special discounts for bulk purchases, please contact Simon & Schuster Special Sales at 1-866-506-1949 or business@simonandschuster.com.

The Simon & Schuster Speakers Bureau can bring authors to your live event. For more information or to book an event, contact the Simon & Schuster Speakers Bureau at 1-866-248-3049 or visit our website at www.simonspeakers.com.

Interior design by Kellie Emery
Images © 123RF/mikabesfamilnaya

Manufactured in the United States of America

1 2023

Library of Congress Control Number: 2023939070

ISBN 978-1-5072-2109-9
ISBN 978-1-5072-2110-5 (ebook)

Contents

Acknowledgments

Dawn Emerick

Marco Constantini

Jenni Murphy

Rose Lavan

Kara Kirby

Sequoia Owen

Michelle Strassman

Ruthie Bowles

NaTasha Jordan, PhD

Chris Cotteta

Dave Gloss

Ryan Daly

Lauren Mudrock

The Trevor Project

National Education Association

Introduction

What would it look like to be happy at work? Your boss would be open and supportive, you and your colleagues would cooperate and have access to high-quality resources, and the organization itself would operate with strong, healthy values. Is that even possible?

Yes.

Employees are starting to push back against unhealthy workplace practices, and companies have to change or risk losing top talent. If you are a manager in an environment filled with an endless calendar of meetings, pointless processes, and a complete lack of appreciation for diversity, don't despair. *Happy at Work* will help you be part of the solution by implementing changes big and small that can improve company culture, boost morale, and enrich employees' experiences.

In this book, you'll find one hundred activities that you can do right now to help build a workplace where employees can feel safe, respected, valued, and, well, *happy*. And as we all know, happy employees are more productive, less likely to quit, and better poised to make your team and company successful. These aren't superficial tips about company swag or mandatory happy hours. These are foundational changes that will help you reform your organization at every level. For example, you'll learn how to:

- Actively listen to your employees' needs
- Give your people real support by following through on requests
- Cut down on needless bureaucracy
- Respect and accommodate diverse needs
- Cultivate genuine work-life balance

- Prioritize mental health
- Advocate for what's right
- Make systemic changes that matter

Whether you're a new leader, an HR warrior, or a visionary CEO, this book will help you focus on what matters (and forget about what doesn't). Through both small changes, like adjusting meeting schedules, and long-term goals, like reducing your company's carbon footprint, you *do* have the power to improve your company culture. It's time to evolve your personal leadership style so you can create an environment where your employees can truly feel *Happy at Work*.

How to Use This Book

The next decade is going to require a lot from leaders. You'll have to navigate flexible work arrangements, economic ups and downs, and new technology. Through it all, *Happy at Work* can help you face and overcome these challenges. By picking up this book, you've already shown that you *actually* care about building a positive workplace culture. So take a deep breath, give yourself a preliminary pat on the back, and let's approach this mission with the self-compassion you deserve.

As you dive into this book, first consider how it can work best for you and your situation. We all have different roles—there isn't just one type of leader, after all. Your personal purview might be large or small. What matters is that you find a way to take *real* action. There is always *something* that you can do to positively affect your team and your colleagues.

Here are three ways you might use this book:

The Purist	The Pragmatist	The Problem Solver
Works best for: Leaders who have a strong ability to influence their organization and want to bring sweeping change.	Works best for: Leaders who care about a positive workplace culture, but would rather focus on real change than fighting unwinnable political battles.	Works best for: Leaders who are struggling with specific problems right now and want to know what will help turn things around.
Good news. If you want to take a thorough and methodical approach to detoxifying your workplace culture, this book can be your step-by-step guide. The chapters and strategies are written in a linear order. So, if you can, start at the beginning and work your way through.	Don't want to waste time on certain strategies you know won't work for you or your organization? Take the à la carte approach. Read through the chapters and choose a few strategies that seem most realistic to you. Each entry works alone.	Can't wait? Go to the index and look for the key words that are most directly related to your challenge. You can always choose more strategies later, after you've dealt with your most pressing issue.

All of these approaches are valid. It's just a matter of deciding which is right for you. This book is organized into three parts:

○ **PART 1: YOUR LEADERSHIP:** Become the Leader You Want to Be

○ **PART 2: YOUR TEAM:** Give Your Team Real Support

○ **PART 3: YOUR ORGANIZATION:** Make Systemic Changes That Matter

As you can see, you'll begin by concentrating on Your Leadership. This portion of the book will help you understand who you want to be as a leader.

From there, it's all about Your Team. The majority of this book focuses on how you can support your team because that's where you have the greatest influence. This part is organized into chapters by topic for ease of use, but keep in mind that all of these subjects should be considered in tandem with the others, not as siloed issues. For example, poor work-life balance affects mental health, and pay inequity disproportionately affects underrepresented groups. Your employees are whole people with a range of needs and preferences, so your solutions should likewise include multiple areas.

The final part is about Your Organization. These entries are about taking on the system as a whole—they will teach you how to advocate for what's right and make systemic changes that matter. These are probably the most challenging ideas, but they can also lead to the most impressive changes.

Many of the tips in this book are different from the standard leadership tips you may have seen before. To build a truly happy workplace culture, we can't keep doing what we've always done. Expect to see unique suggestions (stop acting like every little hiccup is a full-blown emergency), ideas that upend traditional thought (ditch branded swag), and tips that challenge the status quo (consider *fewer* stakeholders, not more). Try to keep an open mind when you encounter something that's unfamiliar—challenging yourself and your organization might be just the ticket.

Before we begin, one important note: While some of these ideas can be applied to other types of organizations, this book is about corporate workplaces. Other types of organizations, like small businesses or those in healthcare, education, or nonprofits, have circumstances and realities that are very specific to them. It may be possible to adapt many of these ideas to fit those environments. However, keep in mind that these techniques are based on the resources and conditions of the corporate world.

chapter 1

How to Build a Positive Workplace

For years, we've been told that everything is going to be okay. If we just dig deep, get scrappy, and try a little harder, then all of our collective work problems will disappear.

How's that working out?

Spoiler alert: It isn't. Because we're facing some pretty tough circumstances—systemic problems that are deeply rooted in harmful behaviors and beliefs. We all want to think that it can get better if we just try our best, but reality is a bit more complicated than that. Still, there are ways you can help shift your company's mindset and encourage improvements. In this chapter, you'll learn about the past so you don't repeat old mistakes. Then you'll look ahead and learn how to build a positive company environment based on core principles, so every employee can feel safe, respected, and valued.

Everything Is Not Okay (But We Can Fix It)

We've all been in *those* meetings. You know, the ones where you find yourself staring at a slide that essentially says, *Everything is fine! We're all doing great!* And if you're honest, you might think to yourself, *Who is this about? It's certainly not about me and my team. We're understaffed, overworked, and toeing some pretty questionable mental health boundaries.*

Despite leaders' best efforts to *pretend* workplaces are happy places to work, very few, if any, organizations have actually built a positive workplace culture. Why? Because it's difficult! So instead of tackling problems head-on, they spend their time either sweeping them under the rug or addressing them with "benefits" that aren't really meaningful to employees.

So what are you going to do about it?

That's right, *you* have a say in all this. Whether your team is made up of two people or two hundred, you have the power to change your workplace. While many companies think that they dictate their culture from on high, the truth is that culture is created, not mandated. Your *real* company culture, the one workers experience every day, doesn't come from an inspirational poster. It comes from the small interactions, the unspoken expectations, and the way people feel.

A positive workplace culture isn't one where people insist that they're happy *all* the time; that's unrealistic. But it is a culture where people actually feel good most of the time and are encouraged to be true to themselves and their values.

So hold off on sharing another soul-crushing PowerPoint about how great everything is, and instead, get ready to dig into what you can actually do to build a *truly* positive workplace culture.

Bring Your Workplace Into Today's World

We are living in a time of transition in the modern workplace. We're moving from older, more ruthless models to environments that are warm and supportive. You must decide: Will you attempt to continue the old ways of bullying and manipulating people to get them to do what you want? Or will you encourage them to be creative and innovative, then celebrate their successes?

The choice is clear. But where do we begin?

A Brief History of Recent Workplace Culture

In order to move forward, we need to look back and understand the past. What is the current state of workplace culture? How has it changed recently? And where does it need to go?

What Is Workplace Culture Anyway?

Let's begin by establishing what culture is (and what it *isn't*). Because, believe it or not, there is a great deal of confusion. Workplace culture is the environment your employees experience every day as they work within your organization. It's a combination of the norms, tone, and conditions that have been established within the work environment. Everyone, including you, is affected by the culture. And, truthfully, every person also *impacts* the culture, albeit some more than others.

Fancy Perks Don't Ensure Positive Company Culture

Why is there some confusion about what workplace culture is? One reason is that it's been conflated with "fun" office perks that often didn't bring the happiness companies thought it would. In the early 2010s, with the rise of the tech company environment, "culture" started to be presented in a more superficial way, with things like in-office slides, happy hours, and nap pods. Businesses thought that if they could present themselves as "fun," then that would be the foundation of their culture.

What those businesses didn't understand is that, no matter how visually impressive the "fun" office looks, no amount of sugarcoating can cover up the *real* company culture. If you're asking your employees to exhaust themselves with seventy-hour workweeks, that is in direct conflict with the "fun" culture you claim to have. By the mid-2010s, this contradiction started to become increasingly apparent. Big, well-funded businesses continued to offer over-the-top employee perks (beer bicycle, anyone?). Companies that didn't have the money for big, shiny amenities still got in on the game where they could, squeezing a Ping-Pong table into the office kitchen and handing out endless branded pens.

Despite the flashy perks, employees at these companies didn't report that they *felt* like they were having a good time when they were surveyed. They said they felt trapped and overworked. Sure, your fancy tech company is offering free dinner if you stay until 7 p.m. But who wants to stay until 7 p.m.?

The Dangers of "Doing More with Less"

Something else was also being introduced at the same time as all of these superficial amenities. You might have heard it called "grit" or "getting scrappy." It was the "do more with less" movement. Things were never the same after the massive layoffs the US economy saw in 2008. Businesses cut positions and resources, yet they still continued to attempt to make record profits. This push strained the physical and mental energy of anyone left at the company. It was essentially a social experiment to see just how much they could cut and still look good on paper. To make matters worse, this movement disproportionately impacted marginalized people.

The "do more with less" movement took many forms:

O We saw a slew of predatory intern programs so exploitative they had to be outlawed.

O Millennials entered the workforce with more student debt than any previous generation.

O Businesses knew they had millennials hamstrung, so they were asked to do more work for less pay or were compensated with "experience" and "opportunity."

O Suddenly, high-deductible healthcare plans were the norm.

O Raises and bonuses disappeared or changed shape. Sure, you could bring your dog to the office...but don't expect more than a 1.5 percent raise. Oh, and here's this year's bonus: a *very* nice company-branded fleece (you weren't expecting actual money, were you?).

Meanwhile, a brigade of bosses began tap dancing their way through phony town hall presentations and "all hands" calls. "Thank you so much for your dedication, and also, no, we won't be replacing Melissa. Can you please pick up her workload?" It was unsustainable, and it didn't take long for cracks to start forming in the system. In the better scenarios, middle managers were simply doing the best they could with limited resources and power. But in the worst, autocratic bosses started shamelessly gaslighting workers into thinking a seventy-hour workweek was normal. Even when the economy began to improve—substantially—it didn't *feel* that way to most people. It felt like they were burned out and still couldn't afford basic necessities.

The "Culture Fit" Excuse and the Great Resignation

As the economy bounced back, many companies expected people to immediately be happy. But if you weren't happy with the unrealistic demands your company was forcing on you, you were probably labeled "difficult." Instead of being taught how to set realistic workloads and timelines, managers were taught how to encourage "resilience." Orders came from on high to make it work, and "pumping up the team" became a core job responsibility for managers.

By the late 2010s, "culture" had never been talked about more. But it was being used as a buzzword. It was even weaponized against employees, who were told that if they couldn't be a "team player," then they weren't a "culture fit."

And then 2020 came along, bringing the pandemic with it.

By this time, the burnout and exhaustion were already rampant. People were running on fumes. So when they were asked to work their way through a massive global crisis, they simply ran out of faith in their employers (if they hadn't already). Employees lost their patience waiting to be paid fairly for the work they were doing or refused to keep working for a company whose values didn't match theirs. Thus, the Great Resignation began. Most corporate businesses were already operating remotely, giving employees more options than ever before. Suddenly, people were no longer limited to joining the companies located in their backyard. They could search for work anywhere, comparing offers and taking the best one. Employees began using the "free market" and "competition" to their advantage, just like companies had been doing for decades.

In addition, the gig economy boomed, giving employees yet more employment options. It had already strongly established itself thanks to new technology platforms that allowed people to quickly and easily offer their services.

Social Justice Causes Take Center Stage

The year 2020 also brought the brutal murders of George Floyd and Breonna Taylor. Violent, racist crimes against Black people certainly weren't new, but they were now publicized more widely via videos and social media. Suddenly, business after business lurched forward to raise their hands and claim that they were part of the solution. They put out statements and made social media posts supporting equality and change. Many businesses thought these bold statements would be enough to satisfy the public demand for companies to support justice. But this time, it wasn't. While representation and commitment to Equity, Diversity, and Inclusion improved, many of these causes and programs were quickly pushed to the back burner once it became time to get "back to work." Employees noticed and called them out on it.

Remote versus In-Office Work

When the pandemic began to wane and occupancy bans were lifted, some CEOs began demanding that workers return to the office. They claimed that they wanted people to come back "for the culture" and "for productivity," which were both proven to be false claims. (According to many studies, employees *can* maintain a company culture and be productive while working remotely.) Employees had experienced a new level of work-life balance, and they didn't want to go back to the way it used to be.

What's Next?

All of this background is important because it helps you understand employees' current state of mind. People have been through the ringer. Even new graduates, who are just entering the workforce and are supposed to be filled with vigor and optimism, are already burned out. After all, they just had to teach themselves a bachelor's degree largely online.

Eustress and Distress in the Workplace

All of these workplace issues in recent years have one thing in common: They are caused by stress. Somewhere along the way, bosses seem to have gotten the idea that, in order to get the best out of people, they need to *squeeze* every drop out of them, causing a ton of stress. It's possible that this was true at some point. Or, rather, that it was a commonly accepted practice that was good enough for the time. The problem is people are not operating from a healthy baseline. So all of that pushing and squeezing is doing serious damage.

Eustress versus Distress

The theory of squeezing workers comes from the concept of eustress and distress.

- **Eustress is healthy, positive stress.** Like when you feel a sense of maximum productivity just in time for a deadline. You may also experience eustress when you're solving a challenging problem or attempting something for the first time. People even experience it when they do a thrilling activity—that little adrenaline boost can be fun and exciting as long as you feel safe while it's happening.

- **Distress is unhealthy stress.** When most people think about distress, they actually are thinking of *extreme* distress. This is something like having a panic attack or becoming overwhelmed by anxiety. However, distress doesn't have to be extreme for it to be unhealthy and unproductive. The moment you go from feeling good to feeling bad, you've crossed from eustress to distress.

Think about the people on your team. People have big, full, demanding lives. They have families to care for and constant societal pressures to endure. Their baseline stress level is probably already pretty high. They're managing to stay in the eustress zone, but just barely. (For some, the baseline is probably already in the distress range.)

Then you come along and start squeezing them. Can they complete that big project by an ultraquick deadline? What about these two new priorities that need to be done today? You can see how it won't take much to nudge employees into distress.

Bosses who do this often *think* they're doing the right thing, motivating employees to give as much as they can. But they're actually making the work harder and increasing stress levels. Think about it: Have you ever seen a boss come along and try to *alleviate* the pressure instead of *causing* it?

Use Your Power to Alleviate Stress

This playbook needs to flip. Instead of your default as a manager being to pour the pressure on, it probably needs to be to help take it off.

Let's also remember that people put a tremendous amount of pressure on themselves. They want to do a good job, and they challenge themselves when they can. But they have so little left in their emotional reserves. If you can help them by giving them more time or an opportunity to focus, they're more likely to be able to successfully manage their stress levels.

Safe, Respected, Valued: A Real, Positive Platform

People produce their best work when they feel good. They'll be happy and you'll be happy. It's a win-win scenario that's actually possible to achieve...*if* you're brave enough to try something different.

So what does it take for people to feel good in their jobs? Here's a hint: It isn't lunchtime pizza parties or company swag. Those are just little Band-Aids that help companies feel like they're making real changes. But you can't take shortcuts to a positive work environment. It has to be real.

In order to feel good at work, people need to feel safe, respected, and valued. These three tenets of a healthy, happy workplace should be what you focus on as you build relationships with your employees:

1. **Feeling safe:** A feeling of security and belonging
2. **Feeling respected:** A core feeling of dignity and recognition
3. **Feeling valued:** A feeling of appreciation and worth

Of course, these tenets are subject to personal preferences and needs. One person's definition of safety will look different from another's, and what makes one person feel respected might not work for someone else. Be sure to communicate with your employees to see how they define these three tenets so you can support and encourage them in personalized ways.

This book covers one hundred actions you can take to build an authentically positive workplace culture. Some ideas are big; some are small. Some are quick and easy to implement; some will take more time and effort. They are wide-ranging. But, in the end, they *all* come back to allowing people to feel safe, respected, and valued. Each entry focuses on one of the three tenets—for example:

- Engage with Our Healthcare Problem: Safe 🔒
- Accommodate Enthusiastically: Safe 🔒
- Be a Good Listener: Respected 🤝
- Invest In Support: Respected 🤝
- Never Pay Below the Median: Valued 🏅
- Recognize Effort, Not Just Results: Valued 🏅

The next time you meet someone who either has very positive or very negative feelings about their job, ask them three questions. Do you feel safe? Do you feel respected? Do you feel valued? Odds are that the happy person will say yes and the unhappy person will say no. These are the things people need to feel good in their jobs and at their workplaces.

If people aren't able to feel safe, respected, and valued, it doesn't matter what else you do: You're never going to have a *real*, positive workplace culture.

Even though each entry in the next ten chapters focuses specifically on one of the three principles, try to keep them *all* in mind as you go about your day-to-day work. Remember, your *real* business culture is the culmination of how your people feel. A positive workplace culture isn't one where people plaster on a fake smile and act happy all the time. It's one where they actually feel good. In each of the one hundred entries in this book, you'll learn what the challenge is, how it makes people feel, and what you can do about it. With some time and practice, you'll find that these three tenets become central to your management style and will help you develop into a more compassionate, thoughtful, and successful leader.

part one

YOUR LEADERSHIP

Become the Leader You Want to Be

We've all heard it before: People don't quit jobs, they quit managers. A dream role can sound perfect on paper. But if the boss is a monster, then the job will probably be a nightmare.

That's where you come in. As a leader, you have tremendous influence on your environment. That's true if you're an aspiring leader, a CEO, or something in between. Your sphere may be large or small but you matter. You set the tone for your team. You determine whether your organization will have a positive, healthy workplace culture or a toxic, stifling workplace culture.

Some policies or work conditions may be outside of your control. But you can always work on yourself and evolve your leadership. Even if your organization isn't ready for change, you can be. You can expand your knowledge and improve your range of leadership skills.

Many leaders are selected for advancement because of their technical expertise. But not only does a good leader need to know what they're doing; they also need to know how to support people. Because that's what leadership is all about: the people and the team. That's complicated because people aren't predictable. You can't just make a few small changes and call it a day. You have to be in tune with their needs so that you can truly work with them.

In this part of the book, you'll find ten ways to become a better leader. You'll learn how to define your leadership values, how to lead with humility, and how to best serve your team. Each topic will help you grow into the best version of yourself so that you can be the leader your team needs.

chapter 2

Evolve Your Leadership Skills

Leaders need a variety of skills: They need technical expertise, they need organizational expertise—but, most importantly, they need people skills. That means the ability to unite people, build up their confidence, and help them reach their potential. Many of the skills that leaders need now are different from the skills leaders needed in the past. The "command and control" style of the twentieth century has no place in the modern corporate world. Organizations are now more matrixed (as opposed to hierarchical—they are decentralized and departments are interconnected), flatter, and operate at a furious pace. That means that you need to be a leader who empowers a strong, confident, nimble team. You can't do that by giving orders or making cuts. Instead, your relationships with your team members should be built on a foundation of respect and trust. To do that, you need to be a great listener and exercise humility. Don't pretend to have all of the answers—everyone knows that you don't.

This chapter will teach you how to prepare for the next era of leadership. You won't find buzzwords like "strategy" and "efficiency" here. Instead, you'll learn about the human side of leadership and learn how to identify your values, admit your mistakes, and care about the right things. Each of these entries offers suggestions and solutions based on empathy and humility. Because, as you carry the mantle of leadership, you'll need to be able to relate to, learn from, and trust your team members.

01. Know Your Values

Help People Feel: *Safe*

Harmful Habit: *Inconsistent, Unclear Values*

Successful Strategy: *Strong Values That Build Trust*

What's Gone Wrong

Here's a *big* secret: There is one thing that sets great leaders apart. It differentiates highly respected leaders from those who are untrustworthy. It can (and *should*) be the foundation of your leadership style too. What's the magic key? Personal values.

In general, people with well-defined values have more fulfilling careers, healthier relationships, and experience more joy. A leader with well-defined values knows who they are. They consciously make decisions based on those values and their integrity is unimpeachable.

Leaders without solid values, on the other hand, are frustrating to work with: One day they're telling you that there's no budget, and the next they're splurging on something that seems unnecessary. This type of inconsistent and erratic behavior is made possible by weak or undefined values. They don't know what they stand for, and, as a result, they make seemingly irrational decisions that confuse their colleagues. At worst, their decisions can be seen as greedy or opportunistic, and at best, they're unreliable and upsetting.

Here's What to Do

Most companies have clear and defined values (even if they aren't particularly authentic)—they are probably outlined in the company's mission statement. But most *people* do not. Fortunately, there is a tried-and-true process for defining your values. Once you take the time to identify which values are most important to you, they can become touchpoints that you can return to again and again throughout your career. Here are the steps to defining your values:

1. Find a list of personal values.
2. Look through the list and mark all of the values that elicit a positive emotional response in one color. Mark the values that elicit a negative emotional response in a second color.
3. Looking back at your list, choose your top five positive and five negative responses. These are your personal values and your opposing values.
4. For each value, take some time to write down what it means to you. What does it look like in real life?
5. Put your values list someplace where you will see it every day, like in your workspace.
6. Take some time to think through how you want to live these values. What will it look like? How will you know that you've been true to yourself?

Here's an example of what your list could look like:

Positive Value: Integrity
What It Means to Me: Standing up for what's right, no matter the cost.
Negative Value: Selfishness
What It Means to Me: Putting one person's needs above all others.

This process can take anywhere from an hour to several days, depending on your preferences. Many leaders later say that taking time to define their values is one of the most impactful personal development exercises they ever completed. Your values list is like a personal compass that will help you feel true to yourself. No one can define your values but you. They're just as unique as your personal background and goals.

Take Action

Good leaders have well-defined values. Take the time to select and define your values—consciously choose what you stand for and what you stand against. You'll find the task personally fulfilling, and it will inspire trust and confidence from those around you. Be sure to look at your list often and check in with it periodically to see if it needs updating.

02. Care (About the Right Things)

Help People Feel: *Respected*

Harmful Habit: *Working under a Selfish Leader*

Successful Strategy: *Working under a Leader Who Cares*

What's Gone Wrong

Leadership is all about people. If you're going to be in a leadership role, that means that most of your time will be spent supporting others. Will it be important to also provide guidance and expertise? Yes. But the most essential part is helping others find their voice and their strength as you build their confidence and allow them to contribute and grow their ideas. In short: It's not about you, it's about them.

Why does that matter? Because too many people have gotten into leadership for the wrong reasons. Maybe they're in it for the better status, higher salary, or a tenacious desire to reach "the top"—without knowing if that's where they are really the happiest. What's ironic about this is that leaders are nothing without their team members. A fancy title and cushy salary may give you status, but it won't make you a leader. Your people skills—and caring about the right things—will.

Here's What to Do

Instead of pushing for leadership roles just for the money or reputation, think about whether you are really well suited for that position.

Ask yourself, are you prepared to:

- ○ Bring people together to help them develop ideas
- ○ Mediate interpersonal conflicts
- ○ Help others grow in their careers

If those are the things you care about, you're fit for leadership. The best leader isn't always the person with the best ideas. It's the person that helps a group arrive at great ideas and gives them the tools they need to bring those ideas to life.

As a leader, it's your job to build a structure that supports and empowers your team, uniting them for a common purpose. People want the work they do to *matter*. That means it should amount to something. If it doesn't, it can be very deflating. In recent years, "purpose" has become a leadership buzzword. However, like so many other buzzwords, it's been weaponized to try and squeeze people and make them work harder. Work should have a purpose, but it doesn't have to *be* your purpose.

If you're focused on your people, you'll bolster them and lift them up on your shoulders. And you'll do it because you truly care about them and the good work that you can do together.

Take Action

Yes, leadership gives you power. You must decide what you're going to do with it. Will you use it to pad your bank account and resume? Or will you use it to improve the experiences of those around you? Leaders spend most of their time supporting others—doing things like helping them develop their ideas, solve problems, and secure the resources they need to grow. If you want to be a good leader, you have to genuinely care for those around you. They are valuable, important members of your team, and it's your job to help them unlock their potential.

03. Assume Good Intentions

Help People Feel: *Respected*

Harmful Habit: *Suspicion and Resentment*

Successful Strategy: *Listening with Positive Intent*

What's Gone Wrong

Have you ever worked for a boss that was exceptionally suspicious? They probably always needed to know where you were and what you were doing and didn't fully trust anything they weren't personally involved in. If so, you probably found the experience to be exhausting and infantilizing.

Too many leaders are deeply suspicious. They act like they're expecting to be tricked or taken advantage of at any moment. They may excuse this behavior by saying it makes them shrewdly aware of everything going on. But it actually reveals a major failure. They didn't build a team that has foundational trust.

Suspicion and mistrust spread like viruses. If a boss is constantly treating their direct reports like liars, it puts everyone into defensive positions. Workers worry constantly that they will be blamed or accused of something. They start protecting themselves and their work, and they're quick to whip out receipts at the earliest sign of trouble. It creates an extremely stressful work environment.

This mindset is what happens when you operate in bad faith. It is impossible to have a positive workplace culture in these conditions.

Here's What to Do

If you are someone who tends to be suspicious (be honest), you almost certainly have reasons for that: You've probably seen people do things in the past that have put you on permanent red alert. Those experiences are valid. However, you should carefully consider how that perspective is negatively affecting everyone around you. Why would anyone trust you if you can't trust them?

It's time for a fresh perspective. Instead of dragging your baggage with you, remember that this is your team, and you are responsible for the people on it. If you haven't assembled a team of people you know you can trust, then don't do anything else until you have. Building a strong team with the right people on it is difficult, but it's your most important job as a leader. Once you do have a solid team in place, good faith is a must. If you want creativity, teamwork, and a positive culture, you have to operate in good faith.

But what if it is a team member or one of your peers who's suspicious, not you? This is a situation where you can use your influence to suss out the root of the issue and try to fix it. If someone is frequently being extremely suspicious or accusatory (we're not talking about things like microaggressions—see #65: Acknowledge Microaggressions in Chapter 8 for more information on how to handle those situations), sit down with them and ask them why. They have probably had some bad experiences too. Or they've been taught to operate that way. Ask them if they can try approaching new situations in good faith, and support them as they attempt to do so. Once you've set expectations, maintain those boundaries and hold your peers accountable for healthy, respectful behavior. Make it clear that you will not tolerate bullying or slander.

Keeping your finger on the pulse of your team's level of trust is especially important when conflicts arise or during times of high stress. Those scenarios put people into distress (see Chapter 1 for more information) and "fight, flight, or freeze" mode. And it's very common to fight with bad faith tactics like finger-pointing or refusing to compromise. If you notice those things happening, slow everything down and help your employees approach the situation in good faith by staying calm and open-minded. You'll find that in most situations, the conflict has been caused inadvertently by misunderstandings or frustrations about other things.

Take Action

You can't have a happy, healthy culture if employees are on the constant lookout for malicious behavior. If you're suspicious by nature, you are probably damaging your team's culture. If you or your colleagues are always pointing fingers, the team is going to get nowhere fast. Slow down, defuse the emotional charge, and remember that instilling trust is one of your most important responsibilities as a leader.

04. Stop Micromanaging

Help People Feel: *Valued*

Harmful Habit: *Constant, Tedious Micromanaging*

Successful Strategy: *Clear Goals and True Autonomy*

What's Gone Wrong

No one wants to be bossed around all day. And yet micromanaging continues to be an enduring problem in a lot of workplaces. Some leaders claim that overseeing every detail is their way of ensuring great work, but the truth is that micromanaging is the easy way out. It doesn't require much planning ahead, trust, or commitment to clear goals. Instead, leaders just force employees to stay on a strict script they wrote themselves.

When you only tell someone *how* to do something, you cut their potential off at the knees. If they don't know *why* they're doing what they're doing, how can they contribute ideas or experiment with different techniques? All they have to go on are your instructions and your feedback. That feedback is usually not much more than "I like this and I don't like that." Why? Who knows. Micromanagers can't be bothered to define or share their reasoning. They're too busy telling you exactly what to do. This incredibly powerful "how versus why" concept was popularized in Simon Sinek's 2009 bestseller *Start with Why*.

The end result of micromanaging is that employees stop trying to achieve goals outside of figuring out what the boss wants. They don't feel that their perspectives are valued, so they don't waste their time offering new ideas. The entire team becomes dependent on the leader. No matter how brilliant that leader is, no one person can amount to the collective potential of a team. It takes a team to build something big. If everyone is constantly following orders, that will never happen.

Here's What to Do

If you want to build a team of empowered people, you have to actually give them power. You can't fake it. If you tell them you trust them but then insist on telling them exactly what to do and how to do it, they're not going to trust you. Instead, you have to involve them in setting goals, trust their expertise, and be willing to reserve your own judgment when it's not vital to the team's goals.

Here are some examples that show this necessary shift in mindset:

Go from Micromanaging:	To Empowering Your Employees:
"Log all of this data that I want to analyze in a spreadsheet I created."	"We need to be able to predict what's going to happen so that we can be prepared. Here's the data we have—what do you gather from it?"
"Add all of these features to our product."	"Users want to be able to express themselves. What ideas do you have to encourage them to do that?"
"Greet every customer using this script."	"The company wants to help customers feel welcome when they enter. How would you do that?"

The examples in the "Empowering" column allow for people to understand why they're doing something, then use their judgment about how best to do it. If you've done your job of hiring the right people, then that's exactly what you want (and it's *definitely* what they want too). In those examples, workers can improvise and continuously improve. They get to exercise their expertise instead of just trying to please their boss.

Take Action

Too many managers have fallen into the micromanaging trap: They can't stop telling people exactly what to do and how to do it. Working under a micromanaging leader gives people no opportunity for autonomy, leaving them frustrated and uninspired. Instead, work together to set collaborative goals. Then truly listen to them and reserve your judgment so that everyone can flourish.

05. Be a Good Listener

Help People Feel: *Respected*

Harmful Habit: *Selfish, Dominating Discussions*

Successful Strategy: *Active Listening and Responding*

What's Gone Wrong

Good leaders really listen to their employees. It's honestly that simple. Being a good listener is extremely important. Every person on your team has ideas (good ones). Unfortunately, some leaders don't create an environment and opportunities for those ideas to be shared. Or, if they are shared, they're either buried in bureaucratic red tape or simply lost in the barrage of constant overwork.

We've all encountered attention-craving showboats who don't listen so much as just wait for their turn to talk. That is, if they actually *did* wait instead of just interjecting with the first thought that popped into their heads.

The result is that conference tables have become a battleground rather than an incubator. Instead of a productive flow of ideas and support, people end up tearing each other down. By the end of the meeting, the showiest peacocks are practically yelling (and sometimes they even are).

Here's What to Do

Active listening is a skill that you can develop. Just like a good journalist learns how to be a good interviewer, you can learn to be a great listener. To do that, follow these steps:

1. **Pay attention.** When someone is speaking, they deserve your respect and undivided focus. Sure, there are many forces vying for your attention (we're all struggling with that). But the loudest and most interruptive

voice you need to learn to quiet is your own. It's easy to get distracted by your own ideas and experiences. But if you're sharing those too often, you're probably not listening enough.

2. **Ask follow-up questions.** Ask thoughtful, open-ended questions that encourage them to share more. You're never going to find out what you don't know if you don't actively create space for others to share. That's true in a one-on-one setting and in groups.

3. **Be yourself.** Yes, you need to quiet your mind so that you're focused on the other person. But you can't act like a vapid robot either. Respond and listen in a way that feels authentic to you and your personality.

4. **Back up listening with action.** Lastly, you absolutely have to back up your listening skills with action. You can be honest about what's possible and what isn't—but then go out and *actually* do your job of making things happen.

Take Action

When employees feel consistently ignored by their boss, they don't share their full perspectives, and that's a loss for both the team and the organization. Develop your active listening skills and make each of your team members a real priority when you're talking with them. And remember, after you finish listening, get to work and help make their ideas a reality.

06. Be a Servant Leader

Help People Feel: *Respected*

Harmful Habit: *Command-and-Control Leadership*

Successful Strategy: *Leading by Serving Others*

What's Gone Wrong

In the old model of leadership, the workers served the leader. That leader operated with a "command-and-control" style, giving orders and making everyone follow them. The goal was uniformity, compliance, and efficiency.

However, in the last twenty years, as the pace of change rapidly increased, it has become essential that leaders serve their workers instead. Because we live in a more complex, less predictable world, it's much more important for workers to have the ability to be creative, empathetic, and adaptive. Instead of giving orders, leaders today are better off supporting their team, ensuring that they have everything they need to succeed. This type of leader is called a servant leader. Servant leaders teach and mentor, celebrate others' success, and recognize that a team is far stronger than any individual could ever be, especially if that team is well resourced and well supported.

You can tell that many leaders are extremely uncomfortable flipping the script and serving more than they control. They're still clinging to mindsets of the past and desperately try to give orders and force obedience. The result is that they're miserable to work for. They may be in positions of power, but there is a constant struggle between them and their team. We live in a highly advanced, globalized, hyper-personalized world where customers expect to have their needs met seamlessly and immediately. If you have any hope of that happening, you need to craft a workforce that is nimble, thoughtful, and empowered.

Here's What to Do

The first step to becoming a real servant leader is to check your reasons for becoming a leader in the first place. (See #2: Care [About the Right Things] in this chapter for more information about this topic.) If it was for power and control, then you're way off base. If it was to bring people together and make things happen, then you're on the right track.

Next, evaluate how well you understand your team's needs. What resources do they need? What education? How about encouragement and autonomy? Think about both their collective needs and their individual needs. Make your primary goal to remove obstacles and give them what they need to be great at their jobs. Depending on your organization, this may be an uphill battle. But it is the right thing to focus on. Listen, learn, and take action.

A final note: Being a servant leader doesn't mean you're spineless or completely permissive. It certainly doesn't mean tolerating laziness or poor performance. It's actually quite the opposite. Listening to and prioritizing others means you need to set aspirational goals and work to achieve them. It's essential that your team can count on you and each other, and that's done by holding everyone accountable to high standards—including yourself.

Take Action

Employees do not exist to serve leaders. Leaders should focus on serving employees. Spend your time helping others grow. Support them, give them what they need, and bring them together as a team so that they can achieve ambitious goals together.

07. Learn about Trauma-Informed Leadership

Help People Feel: *Safe*

Harmful Habit: *Judging and Piling On*

Successful Strategy: *Alleviating the Weight Someone Is Carrying*

What's Gone Wrong

Often, when we think about how people feel and perform at work, we assume that they log on every morning with a blank slate. We believe that if we say the right things or provide the right resources, then people will be happy at their job. But that may not be realistic. When people come to work, they also still have their families, responsibilities, histories, and all different sorts of struggles. And it is likely that they also have trauma.

Trauma is much more prevalent than you might think. There are different types of trauma, "Big T" trauma and "Little t" trauma. Big T traumas are things that might come to mind first, including abuse, illness, violence, and macroaggressions (extreme forms of racism). Little t traumas are often less obvious but still have a very real emotional effect on an individual. Examples include microaggressions, financial struggles, betrayal, or divorce.

Here's What to Do

Recognizing the prevalence of trauma and the need for compassion and accommodation is called trauma-informed leadership. In order to become a trauma-informed leader, you must go through extensive training to learn how to change your mindset from thinking "What's wrong with you?" to "What happened to you?" Seek out the best available training and information and encourage your peers to do the same. It's all about understanding that your employee is not necessarily "at fault," missing deadlines, or deliberately ignoring directions to cause problems; there's simply more going on in their everyday life than you might see at the workplace. Since you can't possibly know everything that happens in every employee's life outside of work, trauma-informed leaders do their best to approach the situation with kindness, understanding, and awareness.

For example, if you have an employee who shies away from sharing ideas, the non–trauma-informed perspective may be that they are uncreative, lack confidence, or "aren't leadership material." Once you're trained in trauma-informed leadership, you become more aware of the serious, unsafe situations that person may have experienced, resulting in more withdrawn behavior. You may need to make more of an effort to establish a safe environment for that person. In the end, small accommodations may have a huge impact on a person's ability to do their job and whether they feel comfortable in their work environment.

Go from this mindset: **WHAT'S WRONG WITH YOU?**	To this one: **WHAT HAPPENED TO YOU?**
Assuming the worst of people	Leading with empathy
Thinking that others' experiences are just like yours	Being aware of experiences unlike yours and creating a safe space for all
Being quick to judge	Reserving judgment

Trauma-informed leadership is a new concept. Most people, particularly those outside of healthcare, education, and social work, have never worked under a trauma-informed boss. You'll need formal training to become a trauma-informed manager, and it's not often offered outright. You might need to talk to your manager or HR to see if training is available. You also have to understand that your employees may be used to actively hiding their trauma. *Never* force someone to share information that they don't want to share. Instead, build trust over time by showing that you care and that you are a safe person who doesn't exploit others' vulnerabilities.

Take Action

Understanding and accommodating trauma is essential for supporting positive mental health, which we'll talk about more in Chapter 8. Even if you do not undergo the training at this point, simply knowing about trauma-informed leadership can help you treat your team with more compassion. When addressing your employees, try approaching every situation with an "empathy first" mindset. You can become more informed about trauma-informed leadership using resources like those available from Dawn Emerick (DawnEmerickConsulting.com) or the list on this website: https://criresilient.org/training/trauma-informed-leadership-certification/.

08. Admit Your Mistakes

Help People Feel: *Respected*
Harmful Habit: *Pretending Like You Are Faultless*
Successful Strategy: *Taking Genuine Responsibility*

What's Gone Wrong

Everyone makes mistakes—even you. Even your boss. Some people are good at admitting to mistakes and making them right. Managers, as a whole, are not.

At worst, leaders can be self-promoting, cunning, showy, and very good at "spin." They aren't particularly humble. The habit of touting their own accomplishments has maybe even helped them get into positions of power. So they see no reason to behave any differently. Other managers just worry that admitting mistakes will show weakness or mean they'll be punished or even fired.

But *you're* trying to build a positive workplace culture, which means openly admitting your mistakes and taking responsibility for them. The trouble is that, even with good intentions, you may not have many good corporate role models in this area. You've probably even seen some spectacular dodges in your career, with a boss doing anything they have to so that they can avoid responsibility.

Here's What to Do

Admitting to mistakes is a habit you can develop and practice. And it's important to do so because, when a mistake does happen, you might feel embarrassed or upset. Being in an emotionally heightened state makes it difficult to react the way you might want to. Knowing what you want to do in these situations ahead of time can help you respond appropriately.

First, get comfortable with the idea that you are okay with admitting to mistakes so that you don't have to make a split-second decision about it at the moment. You are confident in your abilities and your leadership. You aren't perfect and you don't pretend to be. Fully taking responsibility for a mistake is not a weakness; it's a strength.

It may even help to have a mantra that you can repeat to yourself so that you can be more comfortable. Something like:

○ My mistakes do not define me.

○ I don't have to pretend to have all the answers.

○ I am okay with being wrong and owning up to it so that I can learn.

○ I don't judge others for their mistakes, and I hope they don't judge me.

When a real situation comes up, lean on these mantras to guide your reaction. That means being vulnerable instead of clamming up...which is *hard*. So don't expect to get it right every time. But do your best to own up to the issue, figure out how to do it better next time, and be a healthy role model for others.

Take Action

Good leaders take responsibility for their missteps. When you make a mistake, admit to it freely (see #9: Get Good at Apologizing in this chapter for tips on doing that) so that you can focus on making things right instead of avoiding blame. Let your vulnerability be a strength and model good behavior for everyone else around you.

09. Get Good at Apologizing

Help People Feel: *Respected*
Harmful Habit: *Excuses and Blame*
Successful Strategy: *Sincere Apologies*

What's Gone Wrong

"I'm sorry if I offended you, but you really shouldn't be so sensitive." Wait—hold on—that could be better. "I'm sorry, but I'm not the only one who did something wrong, and I think you should apologize too." Nope, still not there... "Alright, I'm sorry! Are you happy now? I was just trying to do the right thing and now *I'm* being treated like the bad guy!"

Ah, insincere, narcissistic apologies. We've heard them from public figures, business leaders, and (probably) family members too. Why? Because when it is time to apologize, we're often feeling very vulnerable and defensive, so those are the emotions that surface most easily. It's not uncommon to see apologies laced with victim-blaming, microaggressions, and diversionary tactics.

Further, most of us have never been taught how to apologize properly. As children, we are often told that we *have to* apologize, but it is often treated like a "check the box" action. As long as you say "sorry," you get to move on. So we grow up without learning to process the emotions that we feel when we do something wrong. And we certainly don't learn how to stand in that vulnerability and convey a sincere apology.

Here's What to Do

Your apology should be "but"-less. Yes, you read that right. It shouldn't have a "but." Let's look at components of insincere and sincere apologies.

Insincere/Selfish Apologies	Sincere Apologies	Why It Matters
Make excuses or cite others who are to blame	Take full responsibility for the situation	You need to show that you fully understand that the mistake was yours.
Are made while in an emotional state, which can be manipulative	Are made after taking time to collect thoughts and process emotions before apologizing	Your apology won't seem meaningful or sincere if it is charged with negative thoughts and emotions.
Apologize for how the other person feels instead of for their own actions	Take personal responsibility for the mistake itself and any negative outcomes of it	This is blame disguised as an apology, and *everyone* will know that you're not sincere.
Demand/expect immediate forgiveness	Are made because it is the right thing to do	Remember, you are not the victim in this situation and your goal is to make it right.
Include conditions or negotiations in their apologies	Are made freely and openly	Real apologies are given because it's the right thing to do, not for personal gain.

Even if your apology is perfect, it will be meaningless if you don't follow up your words with real action. You need to invest your time in doing what it takes to make the situation right. For example, if you provided incorrect information that caused extra work for others, you shouldn't just provide the new information and carry on. You should take whatever action you can to reduce the extra work, whether that is offering to do some of the work yourself (if you're able to) or offering the skills you *do* have to lessen the strain overall.

Take Action

When mistakes happen (which they *will*), you want humility and kindness to lead the way, not defensiveness and blame. When your team members see that *you're* willing to apologize fully, they'll feel more comfortable doing the same. Giving and receiving authentic apologies will make the atmosphere on your team more hospitable, compassionate, and friendly.

10. Be "Unprofessional"

Help People Feel: *Safe*
Harmful Habit: *Pretenses That Exclude and Alienate*
Successful Strategy: *Accepting People As They Are*

What's Gone Wrong

"Professional" is now frequently used as code for a different word: traditional. Do you have an alternative hair color? Unprofessional. Speak with a certain accent? Unprofessional. Rock a bunch of piercings? Unprofessional. If you look closely, you'll see that the word is rarely used to describe something that indicates a person's inability to do their job. And it can often be code for "other." That is, not a cisgender, white, straight man.

It's actually counterproductive to make people conform to traditional business norms. Forcing people to mask their true selves is a quick way to crush their joy and make sure they feel like they *don't* belong. How can anyone be expected to feel happy in an environment like that? Yet in many industries, these norms are still upheld.

Here's What to Do

There are two key things you can do to be a little more *un*professional, both of which make space for others to be themselves and feel like they are accepted.

Be Your True Self

Do you have a work wardrobe that is different from what you normally choose to wear? It's one thing if your work wardrobe is designed for safety or physical ability, like a jumpsuit or scrubs. But it is quite another if your collection of ties or shoes mainly serve to show others that you're "important."

If your work wardrobe suppresses who you are, then it's time to rethink. Did you come of age believing that tattoos should always be hidden or that the office was no place for open-toed shoes? Unless your job involves running or has safety hazards, those expectations are outdated. It's time to reexamine your preconceived notions to make sure they're not impacting how you present yourself—or how you view your existing employees or even potential job candidates.

Make a Safe Space for Others

The next question to ask yourself is "How can I create a safe space for my team to bring their whole selves to work?" To do this, you could dig a little deeper into ways your company might be limiting that openness. For example, the trend in corporate dress codes for the last several years has been to make them gender neutral and to eliminate anything that isn't specifically for safety or utility. Once you've brainstormed a dress code, ask yourself, "Is the dress code more accessible for some people or groups than others?" If the answer is yes, revise until you can answer no. If you have the ability, review your dress code policy and cut it back to the essentials. If you don't have that ability, then encouraging more thoughtful and inclusive language can make a big difference. Consider the language you're using personally and do your best to be neutral (for example, don't call someone's hair "wacky"). Don't let uninformed judgments slide if you overhear your coworkers making them. They add up and can definitely impact people's happiness.

Take Action

People can't feel like they truly belong if they feel judged for being different. Really take the time to examine your preconceived notions about professionalism and how they might be impacting people in your workplace. Focus on creating a safe, inclusive workplace that does not discriminate based on appearance, interests, lifestyle, and more.

part
two

YOUR TEAM

Give Your Team Real Support

Serving and supporting your team is your primary job as a leader. It's where you're going to spend the most time, and it's probably also where you need the most help. Teams are complex. Not only do you have to consider the needs of each individual, but you also have to consider the group as a whole. It doesn't matter if that team has eight people or eight hundred; there are going to be a variety of nuances and personalities to consider. If your team can work together and learn from one another, you'll be able to build a culture that is positive and collaborative. If not, your culture will struggle and stumble.

The good news is that most teams need the same things: They need to be compensated fairly; they need to be rewarded and respected; and they need the opportunity for healthy, balanced lives. It isn't easy work, but it is fairly straightforward. Work with and for your people. All year long.

Sometimes that task can be overwhelming or get lost in the shuffle. After all, your boss is looking at you for certain results and tasks, and it is easy to get caught up in answering emails and running the day-to-day operations of your team. Too many people in management or executive positions spend most of their time pleasing the people above them when they should be spending their time doing the opposite: serving the people on their team.

In this part of the book, you'll find seventy actionable ways that you can give your team real support. Those range from cutting back on red tape, to diffusing tense situations, to prioritizing diversity. Each activity will make your team stronger, healthier, and more stable.

chapter 3

Provide Fair Compensation and Benefits

If we all had the privilege of working only for pleasure, the world would be a very different place. But most of us are working to support ourselves.

Many job descriptions claim that they offer "competitive compensation and benefits." It's part of the boilerplate template, and it seems to get included whether it's true or not. A lack of pay transparency has enabled businesses to continue to make these claims without ever having to back them up, and to perpetuate discriminatory pay practices.

Have you ever been in a candidate review meeting when the topic of salary negotiation comes up? Someone invariably says something like "We don't want someone who's only in it for the money." They might even call the candidate "greedy" if they negotiate in a way they feel is too aggressive.

If a person's desire for fair compensation reveals their character, then why don't we say the same about businesses? If businesses cheap out on salary, healthcare, and employee development, doesn't it say they're greedy and just in it for the money as well?

This chapter will show you how to use whatever power you have to provide fair compensation and benefits. They're simple rules, but that doesn't mean that it will be easy to implement them—a lot will depend on your organization's structure and power channels. Plus, there's a lot of entrenched, arcane information out there about compensation you'll have to debunk. Despite those challenges, you can make progress toward ensuring your employees are paid what they deserve.

11. Never Pay Below the Median

Help People Feel: *Valued*

Harmful Habit: *Paying Below the Median but Expecting Above-Average Talent*

Successful Strategy: *Healthy Compensation That Matches Job Responsibilities and Market Conditions*

What's Gone Wrong

Compensation is one of the ultimate taboo topics in business. We've been told not to talk about it. Ever. That's a piece of "wisdom" that's been passed down through the ages. In some places, it's actually a fireable offense to discuss pay.

However, like some other "strict" business rules, this practice is not in your best interest. There is no legitimate, nonpredatory reason for businesses to hide salary information. Businesses want to hide it so that they can continue to have the upper hand, allowing them to pay as little as they can with no accountability.

Businesses had ample time to change their compensation practices. What happened during that time? Not much. They continued to tightly control all information so that they could pay people what they wanted to without complaint. Lowball job offers, backdoor negotiation practices, and minuscule annual raises ran rampant.

Thankfully, pay transparency has come a long way recently, and it is only going to become more normalized. Now that people have easy and confidential ways to share salary information (e.g., the Internet), they can do so without fear of immediate retribution. Some states and countries have already passed pay transparency and pay protection laws. But even in places that don't have that layer of legal protection, information is much more freely accessible now than it used to be.

Here's What to Do

If you've been in management for some time, you've probably been taught a variety of pay tactics that businesses use to systemically underpay people (or, at least, try to). For example, some hiring managers will always make job offers $5,000 below what they're willing to pay so that there is "room to negotiate." You need to throw all of that away.

In its place, you can use a much simpler rule: Never pay below the median. Using good data (see #13: Use Good Data in this chapter for more information on this topic), you can know what the median salary is for any job. If relevant, you can even filter that further by industry, location, years of experience, etc. Be as specific as you want, but never pay below the median.

You rarely meet a hiring manager who would say that they work for a below-average company (even though they *all* can't be above average). And yet, because of what they've been taught, they're willing to underpay workers. Even worse, they expect those workers to go "above and beyond" for that below-average salary. If you want average work, pay the average. If you want above-average work, then you need to pay *above* the median. If you feel squeamish about that, ask yourself why. Is it because you've been encouraged to squeeze people and salaries as tightly as possible? A few extra dollars profit isn't worth an unhappy workforce. It doesn't benefit your team and so it certainly doesn't benefit you.

Instead of playing games, stick to this simple rule of thumb. It will keep you and your company honest about basic pay practices. From there, you can take on other challenges, like pay equity and inflation adjustments.

Take Action

Corporate culture is littered with predatory compensation practices. Starting now, avoid the many "techniques" to skimp on salaries. Pay transparency is necessary to force businesses into ethical compensation. On your team, follow the rule of never paying below the median (using good data, of course). Ensure that if every salary under your purview was revealed publicly today, you would have nothing to hide.

12. Check the Scoreboard for Inequitable Pay

Help People Feel: *Valued*

Harmful Habit: *Lowballing, Underpaying, and Taking Advantage of Workers*

Successful Strategy: *Fair, Competitive Compensation*

What's Gone Wrong

Equal pay for equal work. We've been saying it for decades. Every company says that they don't discriminate pay based on gender identity, race, sexual orientation, etc. But that's not what the scoreboard shows.

US EARNINGS DISPARITIES BY RACE AND ETHNICITY

Race	Earnings Per Dollar
White	$1.00
Black	$0.76
Native American	$0.77
Asian-Pacific Islander	$1.12
Hispanic/Latino	$0.73
Multiracial	$0.81

Source: www.dol.gov/agencies/ofccp/about/data/earnings/race-and-ethnicity; accessed April 9, 2023.

Unfortunately, these disparities are even more glaring for women.

US EARNINGS DISPARITIES BY GENDER

Sex	Earnings Per Dollar
Male	$1.00
Female	$0.76

Source: www.dol.gov/agencies/ofccp/about/data/earnings/gender; accessed April 9, 2023.
Note: This survey was based on sex assigned at birth and did not include details on nonbinary individuals.

And, as you would expect, the disparity is even more dramatic for women of color. According to the US Government Accountability Office, in 2022, those disparities looked like Native American women, $0.51; Latina women, $0.54; Black women, $0.64; and Asian women, $0.75.

Those are the facts. Now let's talk about the excuses companies use to try to explain this data—excuses about their salary history or their negotiation techniques or their time of hire. You have to recognize that it doesn't matter what the excuses are: If compensation is inequitable, it needs to be fixed immediately.

The scoreboard here shows national US data, but your company also has (or can compile) data that is specific to its workforce. Each person on your payroll has an associated compensation figure and can be described with key demographics. That information is almost always hidden from both internal and external parties. Sometimes it isn't even collected. That doesn't mean that data doesn't exist; it just makes it easier to ignore.

Here's What to Do

If you can, find out what your company is currently doing with its compensation and demographic data. (It may well be nothing.) If the data "doesn't exist," make getting it a top priority. You will probably get pushback that it is a "legal risk" or that there are "privacy considerations." These are more excuses. If the company has nothing to hide, then why is it hiding?

It will probably take some work to uncover your company's pay scoreboard. But once you do, don't allow there to be any more excuses. If two people are doing the same work at similar levels with similar years of experience, match their pay. Give the person who makes less money a raise, effective immediately, so that their compensation is equal. If their years of experience or performance are not as high as the higher-paid person, then make sure that their salaries are proportional to those differences.

These aren't just individual differences. The factors that typically contribute to higher or lower pay are systemic. Here are some examples of those outdated compensation practices:

- Basing salary on previous salary instead of what a role is worth
- Allowing one person to make more when they do the same job
- Paying more experienced people less than what it would take to hire someone today
- Waiting more than twelve months to review compensation

If your company is using any of these tactics, voice your opposition and make things right.

Take Action

Every business should know what their pay inequities are. Once that data is available, take immediate steps to correct pay as needed. Proportional differences due to performance level or years of experience are acceptable, but disproportional differences or those based on salary history or other systemically harmful reasons are not.

13. Use Good Data

What's Gone Wrong

We know—unequivocally—that women are not paid the same as men, despite the law requiring it being in place for decades. We know—again, unequivocally—that People of Color are not equally compensated when compared to white people.

Despite this data, we're still using the same opinion-based approaches to make salary decisions. There's ten times more effort being put into negotiation tactics than fair pay tactics. And those negotiations positively favor people that are already quite privileged.

The data clearly says that we're not doing a good job on equal compensation. Using the same techniques we've been using isn't going to help us get better. But good data is.

Good salary data helps you compare what is with what needs to be. There are always unique circumstances surrounding each individual salary—for example, when they were hired, who hired them, and where they previously worked—all of which can tip the scales in either direction. Using data mutes those factors and forces you and your company to face reality. It takes the opinions and emotions out of the decision and lets you focus on key facts and figures.

Here's What to Do

First, you need to get access to reliable salary data. You can find lots of resources online, but you'll need to make sure they're reputable and reliable. Here's what to look for:

○ **Where does it come from?** The best sources come from verified, factual compensation reports (including the Bureau of Labor Statistics and Payscale Inc.), not self-reported sites like *Glassdoor*.

○ **How recent is it?** The job market changes rapidly. Even data from a year or two ago may no longer be relevant, so be thoughtful about both inflation and recent labor changes.

○ **How much detail is available?** Factors like race, ethnicity, gender, location, industry, years of experience, and specific job responsibilities are important. Look for a data provider that allows you to see as much detail as possible. If the data is too general, you will miss key points about underrepresented populations most likely to experience pay disparities.

You're going to have to pay up to get access to the type of data you need. If your company does not already have a provider, advocate as much as you can. They may argue that they already have plenty of *internal* data, but internal data is inherently biased. Wider data-driven salary information is a game changer. Don't let your company be left behind in this important crusade.

Once you have access to the data, build it into your hiring and salary review process. Make sure that you're consulting the data *every* time a new job is posted (even if you have hired for the same role recently). Similarly, consult the data when you're planning promotions or changes in job responsibility. Beyond that, check in when there are job market changes that might affect a role's worth.

At the end of the day, we're talking about people's bank accounts. Enthusiasm aside, people work because they need to support themselves and their families. Offering flimsy "reasons" for unfair compensation means your company isn't being impartial, compassionate, or employee-focused, and that's certainly something you want to change.

Take Action

You need a reputable source for salary data, and you need to consult it frequently. Instead of making salary decisions based on subjective or precedential reasons, force yourself and your company to use cold, hard facts. Using good data will ensure that your pay is *actually* competitive.

14. Clearly Define Variable Compensation

Help People Feel: *Safe*

Harmful Habit: *Deceptive Bait-and-Switch Incentives*

Successful Strategy: *Trustworthy Incentives*

What's Gone Wrong

Much has been said in business about carrots and sticks—the carrot as bait or incentive and the stick as punishment. Unfortunately, this philosophy assumes that employees must be teased, taunted, pushed, and prodded in order to achieve their potential.

Variable compensation falls into the carrot category. Variable compensation refers to tempting rewards—including bonuses, incentives, profit sharing, equity agreements, stock options, and so on—meant to motivate workers. That can mean that the worker has the potential to increase their compensation if they work hard and get results. The theory is that salaries and wages can only do so much for motivation, but these treats create more possibilities.

However, in the last several years, the carrots seem to have become more metaphorical. Businesses have demanded outstanding performance in exceptional circumstances. But, when it comes time to pay up, they're suddenly silent.

No one likes to have the rug pulled out from under them, especially not when their bank accounts are affected. Often, these bait-and-switch tactics are being used even in positions where *most* of the compensation is variable. Businesses don't seem to feel much obligation to deliver discretionary bonuses.

And that's the problem. When an organization suddenly changes the terms of variable compensation, they show their lack of integrity. They can give excuses about business performance or economic conditions, but it all comes down to the same thing: deceit. In addition, some companies don't give bonuses—and don't even explain why.

Here's What to Do

While it may feel like businesses can do whatever they want "and there's nothing you can do about it," you can begin to stand up against this behavior. After all, it has further eroded the trust people have in corporations and in their employers, and you're working hard to build your team's trust.

One better approach is to have the company make some guarantees. Instead of unspoken agreements or loose frameworks, companies need to make firm commitments to their employees and actually honor them. Many organizations give bonuses, but they are often not structured or guaranteed. They take a stance that overall business performance comes first. So, even if the employee delivered on all of their goals and commitments, the employer still refuses to pay up.

Going forward, try to get your company to set variable compensation terms in stone. Create clearly defined variable compensation plans and put them into formal agreements. Make sure that the terms are reasonable and nonpredatory. That means that the individual should be able to realistically achieve all stated goals. Another key point: Don't tie these extras to overall company performance, which an average person may not have a realistic ability to influence.

In recent years, businesses have tried everything from refusing to honor vesting schedules to canceling bonus programs. That's why nothing can be left to chance: Make it fair, make it clear, and put it in writing.

Take Action

Variable compensation is often used to incentivize employees and encourage good performance. It can come in many forms, but, no matter what type of compensation it is, make sure it is well defined and fair for your team. Only tie variable compensation to goals that are fully achievable by the individual. If they are successful, reward them handsomely.

15. Engage with Our Healthcare Problem

Help People Feel: *Safe*

Harmful Habit: *Ignoring Healthcare Needs, Leaving Workers Trapped*

Successful Strategy: *Accessible, Affordable Healthcare*

What's Gone Wrong

Healthcare in the United States is complicated, political, and messy. It's full of historical twists and turns that have led us to where we are today. If you're not the HR benefits specialist, then it's not your problem, right? Wrong.

The current state of the healthcare system makes it everyone's problem, especially employers. Whether you like it or not, you've been dragged into this situation.

There are many elements of the healthcare system—affordability, availability, navigability—that make it complicated. But as a leader, there is one you should pay particular attention to. How is access to healthcare positively or negatively impacting your people?

People need to feel a basic level of safety in order to have a chance to be happy at work. Access to healthcare is a literal way to ensure safety in the form of their physical well-being.

Here's What to Do

To start, you need to know what benefits plans your company offers, what they cost, and also what healthcare laws apply to your state (or multiple states/locations if your team is geographically dispersed). For you, healthcare may be a "check the box" administrative task. That's because you can afford it. But not everyone can.

Your HR department should have materials explaining the available options. You don't need to know every detail, but you should know what the cost ranges are and what types of plans are available. For example, if an employee's monthly premium cost is $250, what does that get them? Is it a high deductible plan? An HMO? Sometimes a plan can sound like it's affordable, but that may mean that the coverage isn't very good. You need to know what the reality of the coverage is—so that the next time someone comes to you and explains that they have to miss half a day for a doctor's appointment, you understand that the reason is that they have to travel to find someone that's in the network.

To be clear, you do not need to know *any* personal healthcare details. But you should know what kind of financial burden is being levied on your team. If possible, advocate for the best coverage and the lowest employee costs possible.

Being informed will help you be more empathetic. Many companies are very slow to make cost of living increases, but if you know that healthcare costs are going up 10 percent, doesn't it follow that their salary should change accordingly?

The bottom line: It behooves you to understand and engage with your company's health insurance plans. Your support and understanding truly does make a difference to your employees.

Take Action

Employer-funded healthcare means that you and your business are inextricably linked to this issue. Don't ignore the responsibility that comes with that. Make sure you're informed about the healthcare plans your company offers, including cost and coverage information. Remember that, even if these costs seem unremarkable to you, they could be very significant for others, so consider everyone's salary in tandem with costs. Do what you can to support your team as they take care of their health.

16. Invest In Learning

Help People Feel: *Valued*

Harmful Habit: *Expecting New Skills Without Giving Time and Money for Learning*

Successful Strategy: *Generous, High-Quality, Ongoing Learning Programs*

What's Gone Wrong

Encouraging your employees to engage in ongoing learning should be at the top of your priority list. Most employees *want* to keep their skills up to date, learn new technology, and be at the forefront of their industry. But if they don't have *time* to learn these things, they'll feel like they're stagnating in their careers. And that's when their LinkedIn status gets switched to "Open." Notice the emphasis on time. Yes, you're going to need to build learning into your budget too. But *time* is the precious commodity that will determine whether your employees feel enthusiastic about learning...or not.

The issue isn't usually a lack of training available to employees (although *good* training can be more difficult to come by). It's that your team members' schedules are so jam-packed that training feels like it's just *one more thing* that management is shoving onto their mile-high plates.

Think about it: How beneficial can a class be if you're spending the whole time worrying about work that's not getting done? Or sometimes a person ends up camping outside of their planned training session or conference because something *just can't wait*. It's the same issue that haunts employees using their PTO. If being away from work makes their lives harder, people simply don't want to do it.

Which is a shame because people *do* want to learn. After all, learning promotes confidence, creativity, and it makes you feel good.

Take an employee-led approach. Ask them what topics they are interested in and how they prefer to learn. Usually, leadership (or HR) burrows away in a room somewhere and emerges with a plan no one asked for. If you can, set a budget for each person to use for learning in the way they want. If you can't, then at least set a number of days that they can take off specifically for learning purposes.

If your team is struggling to fit learning in, then you need to reduce their workloads. Here are two techniques that can work:

○ **Set a day of the month for learning.** A "First Friday" approach can work. Set aside the first Friday of the month (or the quarter if you need to start small) as a dedicated learning day. Tell them not to plan tasks, due dates, or meetings for those days. Treat it like a holiday, but for learning. Getting the whole company or team on board makes it much more realistic that each person gets a chance to actually spend some time expanding their brain.

○ **Give them chances to teach.** If you're going to plan a series of learning events, ask if anyone would like to teach a topic. It isn't for everyone, but many people enjoy sharing their expertise with their colleagues. And then their team will know that they're the person to go to when that skill or topic is needed.

If you're ready to take it to the next level, set a goal of every employee being able to attend a conference or course every year. If that's inaccessible to you budget-wise, start smaller with online courses or even high-quality free YouTube videos.

Take Action

You want your employees to be continuous learners, but they're going to need time to make that happen. That's where your leadership comes in. Consult with your team members to find out what they want to learn and how. Make sure there is space in their workload, and, if you can, offer a budget to pay for conferences and courses.

17. Invest In Support

Help People Feel: *Respected*
Harmful Habit: *Skimping on Resources*
Successful Strategy: *Robust Support*

What's Gone Wrong

Toxic businesses have a sneaky trick that they love to use. They create a set of impossible circumstances—like doing twelve weeks' worth of work in only six weeks' time—and they put all of the responsibility for solving this problem on their workers. Then they reinforce that responsibility with ideas like "accountability," "work ethic," "agility," and "resilience." All of which make the worker feel like there's something wrong with *them*, as opposed to something wrong with the situation.

This is one of the reasons the modern workforce is so burned out. They've used up every ounce of "grit" and "scrappiness" they had in their reserves. They've been compensating for impossible business conditions for years. And they're done.

Instead of shirking responsibility, use your leadership power to invest in the support that your business actually needs. It sounds basic, but it's actually a fundamental shift. A well-resourced business has a real chance to succeed, and the people working there will be much happier in the process.

Here's What to Do

If you want a happy workforce that doesn't feel cheated and exhausted, then give them what they really need. It's a back-to-basics approach that will make everyone more successful. This support comes in three basic forms: time, money, and person power.

- **Time:** If something should take twelve weeks to complete, don't attempt to cram it into six weeks and expect perfect results. Give adequate time to do the work well. We've become so accustomed to working impossible timelines that we don't even recognize them anymore. Realistic expectations are actually quite refreshing.

- **Money:** Stop skimping. Refusing to pay for helpful resources or the best materials will give you subpar results. That isn't your workers' responsibility. If you want good quality, pay up. This requires planning because, if you're going to invest fully, you want to make sure it's worth it. So spend some time doing financial modeling, researching, and estimating before you jump in. Once you do, fund appropriately.

- **Person power:** Hire the right people with the right abilities. Don't expect the intern to magically have the abilities of a seasoned professional. Don't force three people to do the work of five. If someone leaves the team, replace them right away. This applies to temporary support too. Sometimes you need someone with a special skill that your team does not have. Other times, you need extra person power for a period of time. Hire transparently and expediently.

Again, this feels rudimentary because it is. The trend of businesses cutting corners as a default is unhealthy for both the business and its people. You can reset those expectations. Also, be sure to ask your team what support they want. There might be important investments your team needs, but you don't even know about them because they feel too defeated to tell you. Their perspective and ingenuity are essential, so take the time to actually listen.

Take Action

It's your responsibility to provide your team with the full range of support they need. They're working every day to achieve *your* business goals—the least you can do is ensure that they have what they need to do that. Be generous with the amount of time, money, and person power that is dedicated to each project or process. Get good, realistic estimates and be thoughtful about what you want to invest in. Give your people what they really need, and they'll meet those company goals. And, if you truly can't secure real support, cut back on the workload until it matches the resources you have.

18. Spy On the Competition

Help People Feel: *Respected*

Harmful Habit: *Willfully Ignoring Industry Standards and Market Changes*

Successful Strategy: *A "Finger on the Pulse" of Trends and Changes*

What's Gone Wrong

Managers and executives are more likely to use their past experiences as reference points instead of what's going on right now. Is the past relevant? Of course it is. But if you don't know what's going on now, you're going to be in trouble. So break out your magnifying glass and your invisible ink and put your inner spy to work.

It's so important to know what's happening in your industry, but many leaders are reluctant to get or share information. It's a very competitive atmosphere, and they feel threatened by others in their industry or role, seeing them as rivals. As a result, they get tunnel vision and miss out on important trends, new ideas, and top talent. For example, instead of taking the time to know what others are paying, executives cling to their own organization's historical and current pay rates. Competitive rates for a role may have gone up 15–20 percent, but they'll refuse to pay that because it doesn't match their frame of reference.

If you don't broaden your frame of reference, you're going to miss out on hiring or retaining good employees. Your employees know that they could go apply for a new job any time they want to—and it doesn't have to be a job with a better title. In fact, lateral moves have become the number one way to get good salary increases.

Here's What to Do

If you're going to claim competitive benefits in your job descriptions, you need to know what the competition is doing. What are the current industry salary ranges for the roles under your purview? Are you paying at the top of those ranges? If you're not, how can you tell yourself you're being competitive?

Don't stop at salary information either. How much training and development is being offered? Are other companies offering rotations or coaching programs? You need to know.

Once you're ready to broaden your horizons, here are three great sources for your recon missions:

- **Industry associations and events:** It's hard to make time for industry associations and events, but attending them can give you a huge competitive advantage. Look for national and local associations (you need to pay attention to both) that are popular with others in your role or industry and join them. You'll get to take advantage of any formal learning they offer, and you'll also get a chance to talk more informally with other members.

- **Relationships within your professional network:** As you grow in your career, try to maintain good working relationships with colleagues, even if you don't work together anymore. This doesn't have to be a time-consuming task. Simply send a quick text or social media message when you're thinking about someone. Share articles you're reading. These little things can keep the relationship going and can prove fruitful if you want information about the company where that person works now.

- **The Internet:** Actively seek out comprehensive research. Use reputable salary databases. Subscribe to industry newsletters (and actually read them).

Take Action

Whether you want to call it "spying" or simply just staying informed, you need to know what's going on in your industry and job market right now. When trends change in pay, benefits, or norms, be an early adopter instead of resisting the inevitable. Your team will appreciate your initiative and efforts.

19. Don't Just Manage, Mentor

Help People Feel: *Valued*

Harmful Habit: *Inadequate Support*

Successful Strategy: *Real Partnerships*

What's Gone Wrong

There is a time for managing and a time for mentoring. Managing is for when you need a prescribed set of tasks completed consistently and efficiently. You want everyone to know exactly what to do and you need everyone to be coordinated. That's a time when excellent management is needed.

If you're leading a project that's more ambiguous, however, then management is going to be a struggle. This describes most modern workplaces, where the pace is so fast and there is so much complexity that everyone needs to be able to think on the fly and make good decisions as they go. That's when you need to have done a good job mentoring.

Mentoring is different from management because it gives the other person in the relationship much more autonomy. Today, there is a constant flow of information at all times, requiring frequent adaptation. Because automation has taken over most of the highly repetitive work, jobs for humans are less robotic than they used to be. Thus, employees need to be able to analyze, assess, and solve problems on their own. Mentoring them can help impart those skills.

Here's What to Do

Your team wants to know that their judgment is actually valued. So instead of "bossing" people around, ask them questions. Asking questions can help people learn to think for themselves and trust their own judgment, and you can use their answers to offer targeted help and support.

They shouldn't be leading questions, which can feel patronizing and passive aggressive. But they should be open-ended and genuinely curious in nature. Here are some questions that excellent mentors use:

The Question	Why It's Great
What do you think we should do?	It encourages them to share ideas that they might be holding back.
How can I help?	It lets them know that they aren't alone and that you're willing to take real action.
Who do we need to get involved with?	It leverages your power and network, getting them wider access and support.
What's in the way?	It positions you and the other person against the problem, so that you can attack it together.
Why?	Sometimes, coming back to why helps give perspective. Don't be afraid to question what is happening and why it's needed.

Many people often think of mentors as people who share their personal experiences. That can be helpful as long as you remember two things:

1. Every situation is different, and the world continues to change. What was possible for you at one time may not be possible now. This is why comments like "When I was your age, I had two kids and a mortgage" are unhelpful and can make the person feel defeated or angry. Don't lose sight of the context around your own experiences.
2. This relationship isn't about you. It's about the other person. Don't dominate the conversation. Ask questions and offer brief, relevant experiences. When a person arrives at an answer on their own, they're much more likely to follow through.

Take Action

People are looking for good mentorship. They key is that it actually has to *be* good. Be inquisitive, not instructive. Ask open-ended questions, then help the other person find solutions. This type of mentoring is invaluable to employees of all ages and useful throughout a career.

20. Do Regular Career Planning

Help People Feel: *Valued*

Harmful Habit: *A Stifling, Dead-End Environment*

Successful Strategy: *Abundant Opportunities and Support for Career Development*

What's Gone Wrong

Have you ever known a manager who was personally outraged when someone quit? Or who considered it offensive to mention working anywhere else?

It's silly to think that anyone is going to stay at the same company forever. First, it's unrealistic. Most people change jobs periodically. Second, it ignores the current reality. According to the Bureau of Labor Statistics, average tenure is only 2.8 years for people in the twenty-five to thirty-four age group:

MEDIAN YEARS OF TENURE WITH CURRENT EMPLOYER FOR EMPLOYED WAGE AND SALARY WORKERS

Age	January 2012	January 2022
25 to 34 years	3.2	2.8
35 to 44 years	5.3	4.7
45 to 54 years	7.8	6.9
55 to 64 years	10.3	9.8
65 years and over	10.3	9.9

Source: Bureau of Labor Statistics, www.bls.gov/news.release/pdf/tenure.pdf.

Yes, some workers stay in one place for a long time—and you should support anyone who is able to grow at your company. But very few will stay for their entire careers. With this data in mind, career planning with your employees becomes a matter of practicality. Would you prefer to part amicably or be caught by surprise?

Here's What to Do

Career planning doesn't have to be scary or taboo. It does, however, need to be frequent and consistent—and it requires trust to work. If you haven't built trust with your team, they will not feel comfortable sharing their real goals with you. Review #3: Assume Good Intentions in Chapter 2 for more information on building trust with your team if needed.

Career planning should take place at least twice per year and as often as every quarter. The world is changing quickly and waiting too long for these discussions is careless and avoidable.

Every person on your team has aspirations for themselves. There's no reason they shouldn't achieve them, especially with you as their champion. Here are some questions to ask in your career planning conversations with them:

○ Where would you like to go in your career?

○ What parts of your job do you enjoy? Which parts do you dislike?

○ Are you looking for new challenges right now or are you seeking stability?

Once you know where your employee stands, you have to give them real support. Are they interested in advancing? Give them opportunities to take on more responsibility and access to the right leaders.

Sometimes you might realize that an employee's best opportunities to achieve their goals lie outside of your organization. That's okay. There's no reason, beyond selfishness, to try to hold them back. You might be able to marginally delay their departure, but it's not worth it—they'll be miserable in the meantime. Nothing is more disheartening than the feeling that there is no place for you. Don't be a person who forces that feeling on someone else. (See #90: Accept Losing the Ones You Love in Chapter 10 for more information about supporting employees who want to leave.)

Take Action

It is no longer realistic or appropriate to assume that employees will stay in their role (or even at your organization) indefinitely. Instead of trying to keep people in place, have open, exploratory conversations with each employee about their career goals.

chapter 4

Give Real Recognition and Rewards

In the wild rush that is the modern business environment, it can be hard to find a kind word for a job well done. Recognition and rewards are more often treated like an afterthought. The real focus is on getting the next job done, not on recognizing the effort it took to do the last one.

This situation is a huge contributing factor to burnout and employee frustration. If you're always focused on moving on to the next task or project as quickly as possible, then it feels like you're trapped on a giant corporate hamster wheel that never stops spinning. It starts to feel like the only reward for doing a good job is more work. Why bother to finish the current project when it means that you'll just get more dumped on your plate?

To add insult to injury, businesses have been making all the wrong moves when it comes to recognition and rewards. They know that they need to honor a job well done—but they don't want to pay up so they will tell you they value you...without actually giving you your role's value.

In this chapter, you'll learn what pitfalls to avoid so you can do it right. Many of these actions are monetary (as they should be—that's what people want most, after all). However, some of these are also behavioral. While good performance should absolutely be monetarily compensated, your actions also matter. With a little effort and an appropriate budget, you can show your team that you truly appreciate them and all they do.

21. Actually Recognize Accomplishments

Help People Feel: *Valued*

Harmful Habit: *Constant Fear*

Successful Strategy: *Positive Recognition*

What's Gone Wrong

What's the opposite of rose-colored glasses? It would be a view of the world that focuses on the darkness...the mistakes and the grievances. Unfortunately, that describes a significant number of workplaces. Problems are constantly popping up and, instead of celebrating when something goes right, we gripe over what went wrong. In particular, many bosses seem to have this worldview. They don't notice when things run smoothly. But they appear immediately when difficulties arise.

When celebrations do occur, they often honor the person who was best in a crisis or the one who worked endlessly. We laud their "dedication" and "selfless-ness." But these aren't real accolades; they're not-so-subtle reminders that the business wants you to give it everything you have. Anything less is simply not noteworthy.

Operating this way, companies act like your good performance is unremark-able as a means of keeping you in your place. If great performance barely gets a nod, you probably won't go asking for a raise or a promotion unless you do something extraordinary. They think this will keep you motivated to go above and beyond all the time to try to reach the next level. What they fail to recognize is that this type of stress has resulted in a completely overstressed workforce that is exhausted and insecure.

Here's What to Do

First, evaluate your current recognition plan. Do you recognize successes at annual performance reviews? Quarterly awards? Inconsistently and sporadically? Chances are your current program has room for improvement.

Now consider what improvements you could make on this program. Remember, if people are continuously doing great work, then they should be continuously recognized for that good work. This should happen in both small and large ways. On the small scale, you have friendly day-to-day recognition. This means thanking people for the work that they do and acknowledging the effort and talent that went into it. On a bigger scale, the most important thing is to ensure that job titles and compensation match performance. This is a job, so monetary recognition is more important than any other form. Additionally, you have to verbally express gratitude for the bigger accomplishments, like good ideas, project completion, teamwork, and smooth operations.

It's important that the monetary and verbal recognition go together hand-in-hand. Either one by itself is not enough. You can't just show your gratitude with good compensation and then never say thank you. Similarly, you can't expect verbal appreciation to take the place of healthy, appropriate compensation.

Take Action

Currently, most businesses are doing a bad job at recognition. They are quick to judge—or reprimand—if someone makes a mistake or performs poorly. But when a person does a great job (or even a good job), no one says a thing. Real recognition should take two forms: monetary and verbal. It should also happen both on a day-to-day, small-scale basis and a big-picture, raise/promotion basis. Recognition in both forms is one of your major responsibilities as a leader. Take that duty seriously and make sure your people are getting the real recognition they deserve.

22. Change Titles and Pay Frequently

Help People Feel: *Valued*

Harmful Habit: *Manipulating Employees Into Doing More Work*

Successful Strategy: *Fair Compensation That Matches Current Job Responsibilities*

What's Gone Wrong

On paper, career progression is supposed to look like this:

1. Get a job (we'll call it Job A)
2. Excel at Job A
3. Be recognized as a candidate for Job B
4. Be promoted to Job B
5. Excel at Job B

However, it is now extremely common that it actually looks like this:

1. Get a job (again, Job A)
2. Excel at Job A
3. Be recognized as a candidate for Job B (or, in some cases, simply have it hoisted upon you as a great "opportunity")
4. Excel at Job B
5. Be promoted to Job B (hopefully)

Can you spot the difference between the two? Many companies now put so much onus on workers to teach themselves how to do their jobs that they end up doing the work—in full—for months before they actually get promoted.

A convenient side effect of this little arrangement? When it comes time for the actual promotion to be awarded, the employee has almost no bargaining power. They're already doing the work and almost guaranteed to continue doing so.

Like so many other unhealthy power dynamics, people have become accustomed to these types of situations and employees accept them more than they should. Here's one big hint: Promotions can be given anytime, not just at annual performance reviews. So how do you avoid these traps and advocate for your team members? By evaluating titles and pay multiple times per year.

Here's What to Do

Let's approach this with both monthly and quarterly plans.

Monthly: Check In

You should be discussing performance and satisfaction (theirs, not yours) with your employees about once per month. If you meet for weekly 1:1s, make the first week of the month your "check-in" week. Here are some questions to ask:

○ How does your current workload feel? Do we need to take anything off of your plate?

○ What projects are you most interested in?

○ What would you like to be more or less focused on?

○ How does what you're doing now align with your overall career goals?

That last one is critical. So many bosses only care about what *they* are getting out of an employer/employee relationship. But a real relationship should be more equally balanced. Employees shouldn't have to pretend like every job is their dream job. By asking about overall career goals, you can support your employee as they move in that direction.

Quarterly: Make Appropriate Changes

You should be discussing titles and compensation about once per quarter. Again, set aside the first week of the quarter for these discussions. *Before* the discussion, make sure you've evaluated the following:

- Does their current job title still appropriately reflect the work they're doing?
- Has the job market changed?
- Is their current compensation equal to current fair market pay?

Depending on your organization, it may be more difficult to push through off-cycle promotions and adjustments. Be an advocate and remind your HR or senior leadership that people are no longer willing to wait months to be properly compensated.

Take Action

Businesses are moving at breakneck speed. Employees are often asked to do more work without any extra pay, leaving them to hope for fair compensation *someday*. Keep up with the pace of change by discussing each person's performance, satisfaction, title, and compensation frequently.

23. Recognize Effort, Not Just Results

Help People Feel: *Valued*

Harmful Habit: *Overworking Your People*

Successful Strategy: *Honest Recognition of Effort*

What's Gone Wrong

Allow me to introduce you to the effort paradox. Theoretically, businesses claim to operate as meritocracies: Results and achievements matter most. But, in practice, that isn't enough for most bosses. They don't just want the results; they also want your time. They want to see that you're working hard. But they don't want to acknowledge your effort. So you put forth all this effort, but it's not acknowledged properly.

Senior leaders with lots of power have been taught—often for decades—that they have to push people harder and constantly demand more. They've learned that comfort is the enemy. And where has that left us? Uncomfortable (obviously).

This situation causes two major issues:

1. Effort is treated like an expectation. There is a lot of pressure for employees to work as hard as they physically can.
2. Effort isn't adequately acknowledged.

Sometimes these situations aren't even within an employee's control. They may have been assigned to a client or project that didn't have a high chance of success. They give it their all, but the situation is ultimately a failure. Their effort isn't any less valuable. Some failure is to be expected and can even turn out to be positive in the long run. It's a difficult situation for everyone involved, so showing your gratitude can make a big difference.

Here's What to Do

Start recognizing, praising, and rewarding effort. It takes a lot to keep a business running and much of that work is unglamorous or unseen. Don't take all of that work for granted; that's a surefire way to demotivate your team.

After all, it costs nothing to say, "I see you. I know that you have a massive backlog of demands. Thank you for giving us your time and your brainpower. I am grateful that you're willing to spend this effort on us."

Here are a few ways to show your gratitude for effort, not just results:

- Say thank you for time spent, whether that's within normal working hours or if it's extra hours.
- Take time to verbally acknowledge the value that the person is bringing to the team.
- When projects don't go as planned, appreciate what was learned (even if the desired results didn't happen).
- When projects do go as planned, recount what people did to make it happen.
- Do these actions in good faith, *not* because you're trying to "motivate" people into working more.

When people see that you respect their time, they'll feel more valued. No one wants to toil invisibly and only get called out when the boss wants them to do more. When you recognize effort, you show that you care. That helps people see that you appreciate both their effort and their outcomes.

Take Action

For too long, generations of bosses have refused to acknowledge the effort that employees put into their work. This leaves everyone feeling jaded and resentful. Make sure your employees know that you understand how effort and positive results don't always go hand in hand...but that you'll support them no matter what.

24. Respect Personal Recognition Preferences

Help People Feel: *Valued*

Harmful Habit: *Impersonal or Inappropriate Attempts at Recognition*

Successful Strategy: *Generously Recognizing Good Work According to Individual Preferences*

What's Gone Wrong

It's 4:30 p.m. in the quarterly all-hands meeting. Paula from finance has just finished another long presentation on company projections. Suddenly, Todd, the CEO, decides that it's time to liven things up. Todd knows he's supposed to recognize positive achievements, and he noticed that Noemi has been working late every day this month. *Yes,* Todd thinks, *this is a great moment to tell everyone how much I like it when they work late.* He's up at the microphone, calling out Noemi's name, asking her to stand up for a round of applause. It's Noemi's personal hell to be the center of attention like this. But Todd doesn't know that because he never thought to ask.

With the exception of monetary rewards (which are almost always appropriate), recognition should be personal. There are many different forms it can take. What works for one person might be a nightmare for someone else.

Because of the way we've been selecting leaders, there are some personality traits that are dominant, and a love of attention is one of them. This leads bosses to make a common mistake: assuming that everyone else loves attention too and wants to be recognized in a very public way.

Spoiler alert: Not everyone wants to stand up and have the whole company stare at them. For many, that can feel invasive, triggering much more cortisol than dopamine. Todd meant to reward Noemi with good feelings. But, instead, she just feels surprised, embarrassed, and upset.

Here's What to Do

This solution is nice and easy: You just have to ask. Don't guess or make assumptions about the people on your team. Ask them what kind of rewards they want.

It helps to offer some options. For most people, getting to choose how to be recognized is a novel idea, and they are probably used to getting no recognition at all. Or, if their boss has taken the time to recognize their good work, it's done on the boss's terms.

Instead, try asking them what works best for them. When an appropriate opportunity arises, ask if accolades should be:

- **Written or verbal:** Some people prefer the privacy or permanence of written recognition. Others favor verbal recognition so that there is an opportunity to talk it over.

- **Formal or informal:** Some employees really value formal recognition. Others may feel that the praise is more genuine if it is presented informally.

- **Private or public:** If a member of your team is a very private person, they would probably want to be thanked discreetly. If you have an extroverted, social person on your hands, they might feel much more appreciated if that gratitude is expressed in a form others can see.

Once you know what your team members like, work hard to honor their requests. Doing what they ask also shows your employees that their opinions are heard and valued.

Take Action

Everyone has different recognition preferences. Don't make the mistake of assuming that others want to be recognized the same way that you do. The right thing to do is ask each person what they prefer, then follow through by honoring their needs.

25. Don't Try to Pay in Experience, Exposure, or Opportunity

Help People Feel: *Respected*

Harmful Habit: *Predatory Attempts to Make People Work for Free*

Successful Strategy: *Fair Pay with No Tricks or Evasive Behavior*

What's Gone Wrong

It is sometimes shocking just how creative businesses can be to find ways to underpay people. They will claim that the mere *opportunity* to do certain work has tremendous value to your career, while refusing to actually pay you for that work. This now happens so often that "experience," "exposure," and "opportunity" are well-known code words for more work and less money (or sometimes *no* money).

It is true that each of those things has value—no one is arguing with that. There are, however, two major problems at play:

1. **Certain bosses have used these labels in completely irresponsible ways.** Getting access to exclusive environments, like board meetings, is a highly valuable experience. Taking over your departed colleague's grunt work is not. For the last decade, we've mislabeled all of these extra, undesirable tasks as "opportunities." They've been pushed onto vulnerable employees who weren't in a position to stand up for themselves.

2. **These opportunities have been broadly used as excuses to underpay people.** Or, even worse, to attempt to not pay people at all. Forcing someone to take on additional responsibilities with no additional compensation *isn't* doing them a favor, no matter what you call it. Even if they enjoy the work, they are still entitled to full monetary compensation that matches their responsibilities.

Here's What to Do

Offering valuable experiences, exposure, and opportunities is fantastic—but it does not supersede the need for real financial compensation. Don't delude yourself into thinking otherwise. So, you need to pay appropriately. Here are some examples of types of work that are often overlooked (and, thus, underpaid):

- Taking on more senior responsibilities
- Dedicating extra time and effort
- Learning and executing new skills
- Elite or "challenging" assignments
- Representing the company publicly

Each of these items has value for the individual. But they also have value for the organization. It's unethical and predatory to attempt to get those services without paying for them.

While making this shift yourself is fairly straightforward, you might find that others are stuck in the past. Admitting that these practices are exploitative might mean admitting that you've taken advantage of people in the past. While prior mistakes can't be changed, they can be avoided in the future. If you find that one of your peers is particularly resistant to changing their mindset, help them see that this is about the present, not the past.

Take Action

Millions of people have been taken advantage of under the lure of "experience," "exposure," and "opportunity." The practice has become so widespread that it can't be viewed as innocent individual occurrences. It's a known predatory manipulation of dangling a carrot without ever actually giving commensurate compensation. Offer as many opportunities as you possibly can—just be sure to offer the appropriate monetary rewards to go with them.

26. Set a Clear Bonus Plan

Help People Feel: *Valued*

Harmful Habit: *Bait-and-Switch Bonus Incentives*

Successful Strategy: *Reliable, Fair Bonuses*

What's Gone Wrong

"In addition to your base salary, you may be eligible for an annual bonus. Your eligibility to receive a bonus, the bonus amount, and the payment terms shall be at the sole discretion of your employer."

How many times have you seen this phrase (or one like it) included in a job offer? It's the epitome of a CYA non-promise. It acknowledges that bonuses exist. Maybe you'll get one! Maybe not. Have fun wondering and please feel free to work as hard as possible in the hope that maybe you'll get rewarded for it.

Bonuses are standard good practice, so many companies offer them. But many companies also reward them inconsistently, which is frustrating for employees. If a business finds itself unable to pay an appropriate end-of-year bonus, it is most likely because of poor planning and budgeting.

Here's What to Do

The keys to a healthy bonus plan are transparency and follow-through. First, make sure that the requirements for bonuses are crystal clear. They should be formally written into either employment agreements or annual goals so that both the employer and the employee have concrete documentation.

Next is the follow-through. Often, companies make the mistake of failing to budget for bonuses. It's an afterthought. As a result, a tiny bonus pool is conjured up out of nothing, and you're left to distribute the crumbs. Don't let this happen. If your company wants employees (or customers) to trust them, then their commitment to delivering on what was promised must be ironclad. Remember, people have worked all year for this. They shouldn't have to wonder if that effort is going to pay off.

Some companies structure their bonuses in two steps:

1. The company must hit its financial goals.
2. If a specific company goal is achieved, then an employee *may* be eligible for their bonus.

For years, people have voiced how unfair this is. Unless your company is very small, most of the people that work there aren't going to be in positions to directly influence whether or not macro company goals are achieved. Employees are still being asked to give their all, but nothing is guaranteed.

Instead, spend more time in your planning process confirming that goals are well aligned and can be met. Be cautious of goals that sound good on paper but don't directly impact the company's success. Those are filler goals. They might be worthwhile, but they should *not* be tied to variable compensation. Here are some examples of clear, appropriate, and influential goals:

Role	Influential Goal	Filler Goal
Sales	Top line revenue	Adopting a new CRM
Operations	Number of units shipped	Automate 15 percent of all operational tasks
Product Development	Customer renewal rate	Number of new features

Again, it isn't that the filler goals don't matter. But they're either too indirectly related to company success (the CRM) or they're too unpredictable (the automation and new features). Good parameters for bonuses should be clear, concrete numbers that actually matter.

Take Action

Bonuses don't have to be completely unpredictable and unreliable. If a business plans appropriately, sets clear goals, and follows through on its promises, then everyone wins. Write your team's goals and budgets in such a way that you can offer bonuses reliably.

27. Give Everyone a "High Potential" Plan

Help People Feel: *Respected*

Harmful Habit: *Limiting the "High Potential" Label to a Select Few*

Successful Strategy: *Helping Everyone Reach Their Potential*

What's Gone Wrong

"High Potentials," or "HiPos," are a group of individuals who have been plucked from the general pool and set on a track for greatness. Potentially.

Many businesses have these "High Potential" programs. Some of them are fantastic, but others cause more problems than they solve. What's the main difference between the two? It's how people are selected for the programs. The worst HiPo programs use one of two methods for inducting new participants: personality tests or manager nominations. Both are deeply flawed and, ultimately, counterproductive—and they are very vulnerable to in-group favoritism.

○ **Personality tests** are good tools for helping individuals better understand themselves. But when used as a tool for selection, they become dangerous. HiPo programs have the potential to diversify your leadership, but personality tests and other similar assessments (measuring aptitude or strengths) actually homogenize your leadership pipeline because they tend to reward certain traits they deem useful. After all, what makes a great leader? It isn't a single set of traits. You want all types to be represented in your leadership, not just those who score high in something like "drive" or "confidence."

○ **Manager nominations** have the same problem. Managers are most likely to play favorites and nominate people who are similar to them. It creates a bit of a self-perpetuating cycle. If your leaders have historically been more dominating, then manager nominations are likely to get you more of the same. That means that you're going to be prepared for the past, not the future.

The alternative is staring you right in the face: Recognize the potential in more people. Offer *everyone* the chance to be supported so that they can grow.

Here's What to Do

The bad part of HiPo programs is their flawed methods of selection. But the *good* part is the actual enrichment opportunities that come with them. Companies know that these work; they just don't want to adequately invest in them. You can't expect to have an A+ workforce with only C- investment. Here are three opportunities typically offered to HiPos that would benefit everyone:

1. **Structured development plans:** HiPo development plans are much better than typical performance reviews. They're usually cocreated by HR, current leadership, the individual, and sometimes a coach or leadership consultant. That level of investment and support from interested parties makes a big difference. Additionally, personalized structured development plans are forward-looking (as opposed to performance reviews, which are backward-facing). If possible, swap your review process for a development planning process instead.
2. **Access to learning:** Continuing education is essential for both individual and organizational success. HiPos are usually given opportunities to participate in more internal and external learning programs. Access to learning can't just be reserved for a small class of elite individuals. Make learning an organizational priority that is accessible to all.
3. **Mentorship, coaching, and shadow programs:** HiPos are often invited to participate in experiential development where participants gain access to counsel, personal support, and opportunities to build relationships. This is increasingly important in the age of dispersed teams because casual interactions aren't as spontaneous as they were in office settings.

These programs require some effort to get up and running but will pay for themselves many times over because they have the potential to make your employees feel invested in and well supported.

Take Action

Separating out "High Potential" individuals based on personality tests or manager nominations is a surefire way to homogenize your company leadership. Ditch the elitism and lack of diversity of most HiPo programs. Instead, take common HiPo enrichment opportunities and make them as accessible as possible.

28. Don't Accidentally Reward Bad Behavior

Help People Feel: *Respected*

Harmful Habit: *Hero Syndrome and Squeaky Wheel Syndrome*

Successful Strategy: *Recognizing People Who Actually Deserve It*

What's Gone Wrong

You know Blaise over in accounting? He's the one who chewed out that whole team of interns last month because they didn't finish their reports fast enough. And back in January he stormed out of a group project because he wasn't put in charge of it. Well, you're not going to believe this, but he's just been promoted.

Actually, maybe you *will* believe it because this happens every day. And it sends a terrible message to your team.

Usually, the "reason" that someone like Blaise is allowed to go unchecked is because he's "brilliant" or at least very talented. The problem is that he is *also* selfish, uncooperative, and cocky, which leaves the rest of the team feeling angry, resentful, and dejected. Why should they bother being respectful, responsible colleagues when someone like Blaise is rampaging his way up the corporate ladder?

Here's What to Do

For too long, businesses and leaders have valued characteristics that do more harm than good. Getting the work done is great, but it isn't worth it if the person in question tears everyone else down on their way. One person, no matter how clever or driven or inspired, is nothing compared to a team. It takes a *team* to do big, important things that matter.

So, as a leader, it's your job to take the team's well-being into account when you consider promotions and rewards—and even continued employment. Stop unintentionally telling your team that bad behavior is acceptable. It isn't.

In organizational leadership, there's a concept called "permission to play." These are the minimum standards of behavior required of any team member. Examples include:

○ Treating all team members with respect

○ Listening to others, collaborating, and compromising

○ Following through on commitments

○ Acting with honesty, integrity, and in good faith

As the team leader, you decide who gets to be on the team. You are literally the one who grants or denies permission to play. It's one of your most essential responsibilities. If you allow someone to violate these values but still remain on the team, you're granting them permission to do so.

Instead of accidentally rewarding bad behavior, address it right away. Define your "permission to play" values, then share them with your team so everyone is on the same page. Make it clear that meeting those standards is foundational to being part of the team. If needed, back this message up with disciplinary action.

Take Action

We often are willing to tolerate disrespectful behavior from certain "brilliant" individuals. But allowing one person to behave selfishly is frustrating and demoralizing for everyone else on the team. When evaluating performance (and particularly when deciding who to promote), consider a person's corporate citizenship, not just their skills or results. One bad actor can diminish everyone around them. It's your job as a leader not to allow that to happen, even if it's happened in the past.

29. Encourage Peer Recognition

Help People Feel: *Valued*

Harmful Habit: *Jealousy and Unnecessary Competition*

Successful Strategy: *Positive Peer Support*

What's Gone Wrong

Your relationship with your people is important. But so are their relationships with each other. Do they support and celebrate each other? Or do they devolve into jealous sniping and finger-pointing? Either way, it says a lot about their environment.

You can't (and shouldn't try to) control anyone. But you can create and control the conditions that influence your team's behavior. If you have a high-pressure, every-person-for-themself environment based on fear, you're very likely to get back-stabbing, grudge-holding, and all-out nastiness.

Conversely, if you create an environment where the people on your team are caring, gracious, and depend on one another, you're likely to get happier employees. Sure, a little competitive spirit can be healthy and beneficial. But, at the end of the day, you want your people to compete as a *team*.

Here's What to Do

Peer recognition should be both formal and informal—and it should be genuine. This is something that you can both model yourself and encourage in others.

Hire the Right People

This is one of the most important factors that will determine the culture of your team. Yes, you need people who are talented. Yes, you need people who are hardworking and innovative. But it is just as important that they are kind, collaborative, humble, dependable, and trustworthy.

Often when businesses talk about "culture fit," they do so in a superficial way. Respect is something that is nonnegotiable. If you've done your job in hiring the right people to be on the team, they'll be very forthcoming with praise for their colleagues. You should be evaluating humility and the ability to collaborate when interviewing for all positions.

Build a Peer Recognition System

It's not enough to just have excellent people and good intentions. Organizations are made up of systems. Those systems help to channel the raw energy on your team to create a more consistent environment.

There are a lot of options for peer recognition systems. Some of them are simple recognition boards; others use sophisticated points systems that can be exchanged for prizes or even cash. Make this an organizational habit that is easy to use. Then use it liberally and encourage others to do the same.

Make It Meaningful

Most organizations prioritize manager reviews over peer recognition. They do this despite the fact that most managers are inevitably biased. Peers have a very important perspective of one another, and they always know who the real "team players" are. So don't dismiss their recognition of one another.

For example, when new positions open up within the company, is there a simple, widely used way for employees to nominate their colleagues? If someone is frequently recognized by their peers, does that factor into their annual raise? It should. Many vantage points are better than just one. Pay attention to what is being said and tie that recognition back to real, monetary awards and advancement opportunities.

Take Action

Working on a team of backstabbers is exhausting and miserable. You want to steer your team away from potential competitive pitfalls and encourage them to support each other. Peer recognition is great for promoting positivity within your team. It's only possible if you have people on the team who care about more than just themselves. Build the team correctly and then give them a simple but significant way to recognize each other.

30. Debrand Your Swag

Help People Feel: *Valued*

Harmful Habit: *Expecting Your People to Wear Your Brand*

Successful Strategy: *Appreciation Gifts People Actually Like*

What's Gone Wrong

What do a lovely vest, a fancy pen, and a trendy water bottle all have in common? They can all be ruined with your company logo.

Look, there's nothing wrong with wanting to give out some swag. The problem is that companies have been pulling two bad-faith moves for the last several years:

1. They've been attempting to pass off these items as rewards instead of well-deserved monetary bonuses.
2. They've been assuming (and sometimes demanding) that people want to wear or display their brand.

No matter how well intentioned your giveaways may be, people are going to be a little suspicious of them. Because a fleece jacket is not a bonus.

Corporate swag really took off with the tech boom. Maybe it's because the logos got a lot more fun. Or maybe it's that the work dress code got a lot more casual and suddenly it was perfectly fine to wear that butter-soft logo tee on a Tuesday. But, like so many things, it has become oversaturated and overdone.

Here's What to Do

Gift giving should be about the recipient, not the giver. No one wants to feel like a walking advertisement, so why would they want to go around displaying your corporate logo? We've become used to the logo as the price we collectively pay for getting whatever the nice swag items are. That doesn't mean anyone likes it.

Here's an easy experiment. The next time you're involved in any swag planning, introduce an unbranded option. If you can, start at the beginning and just ask how many people would be interested in an unbranded version of the item if it were available. The answer may surprise you.

Because if the swag actually is supposed to be a gift, then the goal is for people to be able to enjoy it. Some people may enjoy the item just fine if it has the logo on it. To them, the logo is neutral and doesn't interfere with their use or satisfaction. But if others tell you that they would enjoy the item more if it was unbranded, then why wouldn't you listen to them? The only real answer is that you *do* want them to do some free advertising for you. Not only is that unfair and unrealistic, but it's also just plain gross.

If you aren't able to offer an unbranded option (probably because HR insists that it isn't necessary), then at least advocate for more subtlety. A small logo is less obvious than a large one. A few other things you can do to make corporate gifts more enjoyable include:

○ Giving an option to take the cash value instead of the gift

○ Giving a range of options for employees to choose from

○ Being size-inclusive for all wearable gifts

These tips can help any corporate swag you do end up making be at least more palatable to your team.

Take Action

Instead of plastering your logo all over everything, either give items that are completely unbranded or offer an unbranded option. Never attempt to pass off swag items as any kind of bonus. Gifts should be given in good faith and without ego or not offered at all.

chapter 5

Eliminate Bureaucracy and Stop Wasting Employee Time

Time is our most valuable resource. It is finite, precious, and nonrenewable. We each only get a limited amount of it, both in the short and long term.

When business leaders make decisions about employee time, they seem to be as cavalier as they wish to be. New time-consuming process? Yes, let's add it. Stricter rules with more red tape? Why not?

There is a strong tendency to pile on with little care for the actual people who will be contributing their time. No one stops to ask if the amount of time spent on a task is commensurate with the outcome. Without that analysis, it's all too easy to add more and more and *more* and thus be disrespectful of people's time.

The most agile businesses are the ones that strip away the time wasters and leave only what's essential. That strategy leaves a happier team that isn't bogged down with bureaucracy. It requires you to be more thoughtful about how you are willing to spend employee time. The goal is to save time for the things that actually matter.

The entries in this chapter will help you rethink some of the bureaucratic roadblocks that are probably eating away at your business's progress. By pulling back on things like unproductive meetings, bloated processes, and low-value distractions, you'll give your team permission to be more focused, autonomous, and productive.

31. Take Prioritization Seriously

Help People Feel: *Respected*

Harmful Habit: *Overloaded Priority Lists That Workers Can't Realistically Complete*

Successful Strategy: *Clear, Well-Defined Priorities*

What's Gone Wrong

Prioritization in the corporate world is a joke. People talk about it all the time because they want to show that they're "strategic" and "efficient." The problem is no one seems to be able to say anything is *not* a priority, meaning everything is in the Urgent category.

When you prioritize, of course, you designate which things are the most important and which are less important. Bosses aren't hesitant to declare tasks or projects to be *most* important; they do that all the time. What happens when you add more and more priorities without ever pulling anything *off* of the list? Your prioritization ceases to mean anything.

Sometimes prioritization is even used as a weapon. Instead of cutting a project from the list, businesses will put the responsibility back on the worker. They blame the worker's lack of prioritization skills for their inability to get all of the work done. They're assigning superhuman workloads and then blaming the workers when they aren't able to keep up—that's unfair and setting employees up to fail.

Here's What to Do

You need to get good at making cuts. The real power of prioritization isn't in what you give the "high priority" label. It's in what you assign the "low priority" label. It's time to proactively recognize that each person can only do a limited number of things (and even fewer if you want them done well).

How do you decide what to cut or deprioritize? It's going to seem scary at first. We're used to saving everything "just in case." But once you see how much more effective your team can be once distracting, low-priority tasks are off of their to-do lists, you'll never want to go back.

Step 1: Define How to Prioritize

What are the most important goals to your company? Are they the projects that generate the most revenue? Or programs that make your team more efficient? Or output that has the greatest impact on customers? Those are sometimes all the same thing, but sometimes they aren't. Pick something clear and concrete.

Step 2: Put Your Priorities in Order

Once you have your list, it's time to rank your priorities. Put them in numeric order—no ties allowed. Make sure you're documenting all of the projects and tasks so that nothing is sneaking in that's not accounted for. Do this task together with your employees so that you all understand what's involved in each project. If you communicate your rationale for your decisions, then they'll also be able to prioritize in the moment if two tasks arise simultaneously.

Step 3: Make Cuts

This is the fun part. There is true joy in saying, "No, we aren't going to do this." As you look over the priority list, you need to pick a tipping point where the tasks stop having a significant impact. You might not want to acknowledge it, but there is a cutoff. If you're having difficulty, start by cutting at least the bottom 20 percent of tasks. If you're feeling truly brave, cut the bottom 50 percent. Remember, for each cut you make, you're going to get more time and focus on the real priorities.

Usually, a portion of the cut tasks will be items that no one misses. However, you may find that one of your peers or team members has strong feelings about not cutting something, even if it's unproductive. Address those concerns head on. You can substitute priorities, but you can't keep everything.

Take Action

Too many organizations want to add "high priority" items to workloads, but they are rarely willing to remove "low priority" items. If you're bold enough to do it right, cutting low priorities is remarkably powerful. Your team members will have more time to do important work well.

32. Take Shortcuts

Help People Feel: *Respected*

Harmful Habit: *Pointless, Arduous Processes*

Successful Strategy: *Constant Streamlining*

What's Gone Wrong

Good news. You have permission to do *less*. Yes, really. It could actually be a huge help.

In the business world, shortcuts are usually regarded as lazy or irresponsible. But if there's a way to save real time, it shouldn't be ignored. Continuous streamlining should be a core skill for you and your team members. Time is a very precious resource. Leaders should *want* people to be hunting for simpler, quicker ways to get things done. You want them to test out as many shortcuts as possible to see which ones may actually be better than taking the long way around. (Nothing dangerous, obviously. This doesn't apply to any type of life-or-death situation. But it absolutely does apply to most corporate processes.)

You need to prune processes like rose bushes. As soon as one becomes unproductive, cut it off so that the energy can be redirected back to the rest of your business.

Here's What to Do

Every manager alive will tell you that efficiency is important. They want the speed and cost savings that come with efficiency. What they don't seem to want is the actual reduced effort. To them, shortcuts can only be bad. But let's look at a sample administrative process, where employees ranked the effort each step required, and how impactful each step was:

Step 1	Step 2	Step 3	Step 4	Step 5
Meeting agenda is written and sent out in advance.	Meeting agenda is reviewed at the start of the meeting.	Assigned scribe takes detailed notes during meeting.	Scribe reformats notes according to prescribed procedures.	Scribe distributes notes to all attendees.
Effort: 3/5 Impact: 5/5	Effort: 3/5 Impact: 2/5	Effort: 4/5 Impact: 4/5	Effort: 4/5 Impact: 1/5	Effort: 2/5 Impact: 5/5

Immediately, step two and step four should stick out as suspect because their effort outweighs their impact. For example, does reformatting the notes have some impact? Yes. But does it justify the effort? Probably not. Be liberal and cut out the steps. It wastes an hour of valuable employee time, and it might not even be needed. You don't have the luxury of that extra time, and your team desperately needs more simplicity. Don't hesitate—deadhead that step in the process and don't look back.

Take Action

As a leader, look to stop adding tasks and instead find possible shortcuts to be taken. Bonus points if you encourage employees to suggest the shortcuts! The goal should be the simplest process with the most effective results. If something isn't worth the effort, prune it immediately to make space for more important activities.

33. Ditch the Decks (They're Bad for Your Soul)

Help People Feel: *Respected*

Harmful Habit: *Obsessing over Time-Consuming, Unnecessary Slide Decks*

Successful Strategy: *Sparing, Appropriate Use of Visual Aids*

What's Gone Wrong

Who doesn't love a good TED Talk? They're like little brainteasers that follow a perfectly predictable formula. There's a thought-provoking topic, a few well-placed jokes, interesting anecdotes, and, of course, a perfectly complementary slide deck. And you know what is particularly great about those decks? Their minimalism. Typically just a single word or image per slide. If only all decks could say the same.

Imagine your team the night before a big pitch....Are they reviewing single-word slides or painstakingly nudging and resizing text boxes so that they can fit just *one more thing* in the frame?

The corporate world has gone way overboard with slide decks. More specifically, we've lost the plot a bit and found ourselves obsessing over the form but not the function. Creating and formatting slides is time-consuming. As with everything in this chapter, they've become just one more thing that sucks up your team's time. The amount of effort isn't proportional to the benefit. Still, we've become so accustomed to using slide decks that we simply expect them to be there.

Here's What to Do

Visual aids can be extremely helpful, so don't dump them altogether. However, invite your team to be more thoughtful about what types of visual aids are helpful.

Now that we live in such a virtual world, visual aids hold an interesting place in our lives. If you attended an in-person meeting back in 2019, you were probably sitting around a big table, facing other participants while the slide was projected in the background. If you were to attend a virtual meeting today, the slide would take up 80 percent of the screen while a few of the participants occupy tiny boxes at the bottom.

Do you see the missed opportunity? We're blunting important occasions to interact. This is especially true if the slide is left up for the entire meeting, even after the discussion has veered away from what is being viewed.

So, if you want to be more selective about the use of slide decks, here are some alternative visual aid options that may take up less time and provide more value:

○ Simple diagrams or images

○ Live documents

○ Virtual whiteboards

○ Video clips

○ Infographics

○ And, of course...nothing!

Naturally, the same ideas apply to all of these types of aids too: Simple is better; less is more. It's easy to get distracted by formatting and layouts. If those things bring the concept to life, that's great. But if they don't, then allow your team to back off a bit.

Take Action

We're overusing slide decks. They're time-consuming to make and they can distract from actual interaction. If you truly need a slide deck, opt for more minimalist slides. Otherwise, consider alternative visual aids or forgoing visual aids in favor of "face-to-face" conversation.

34. Cut Down on Meetings

Help People Feel: *Valued*

Harmful Habit: *Too Many Poorly Planned, Unnecessary Meetings*

Successful Strategy: *Communication That Flows Through Appropriate Channels*

What's Gone Wrong

Could this be an email?

Yes, that's a cliché at this point. You would think that would mean that we know not to accidentally commit this corporate sin. But you would be wrong.

In fact, now that organizations use so many communication channels (email, Slack, texts, CRMs, project management tools, Google Drive, and so on), we are falling into even more communication sand traps. We use so many channels that it's impossible to keep up with each one. Plus, everyone has different communication preferences (see #69: Understand Individual Communication Needs in Chapter 8). One person likes to just "pick up the phone," while another abhors calls. It's a minefield.

And then there are the meetings. We now spend even more time in meetings than we did five years ago. The best meetings are properly planned and actually accomplish their goal. The worst meander about eating productivity for breakfast and chip away at your will to live. There are far too many of the latter and nowhere near enough of the former.

Here's What to Do

If you need a motivator, just think of how you feel at the end of a meeting that was a giant waste of time. Your entire team feels that. It's exhausting. It's worth making the changes, even if it's hard. In order to take your calendar from looking like a brick wall to more of an open window, you're going to need to streamline and standardize.

Streamline

Here's a little trick that works wonders: Make it your goal to have as few meetings as possible. Meetings should be reserved for when they're absolutely needed, especially if they include more than three people.

That's another area that can be streamlined: Who's included in these meetings? Meetings between two people can be remarkably productive, especially when they're spontaneous. Three people? Fine. More than that and you need to be extremely thoughtful.

If you're having trouble, take a look at the regular meetings on your calendar. Leave your 1:1s as they are because those are nonnegotiable. Out of what remains, rank them from most productive to least productive (no ties allowed—that's cheating). Then look at the bottom 50 percent of meetings with extreme skepticism. Put those meetings on notice. If at all possible, consolidate or cut them.

Standardize

It's one thing to change your own habits—but that isn't going to be enough to save your team from "death by meeting." It's a discussion that needs to be had, perhaps frequently. Then try to set some standards for the future.

There's no need to scold anyone for anything that's happened already. Instead, approach this standardization like more of a lifestyle change. You might decide that Fridays are no-meeting days. Or you might initiate a thirty-day low-meeting period. Talk to your team and ask them what they want. Then set some simple, clear standards that apply to everyone, no exceptions.

Take Action

We all know that we're trapped in too many meetings. But we aren't doing anything about it. While it may seem like every meeting is important, there have to be trade-offs. Start by cleaning out your own calendar. Then work with your team to streamline and standardize meeting practices. Your team's happiness and productivity will both soar.

35. Get Comfortable with Automation

Help People Feel: *Valued*

Harmful Habit: *Repetitive Manual Processes*

Successful Strategy: *Technology That Takes the Burden*

What's Gone Wrong

The topic of artificial intelligence, robots, and automation usually brings a bunch of suspicion. But what if we looked at these options as a welcome source of help instead of the enemy?

Let's take time sheets, for example. Humans aren't great at time sheets. They forget to keep them up-to-date, resulting in a scramble to finish and submit them right before they're due. They give inaccurate information based on their memory or impression of what happened (not what actually happened). In short, they're quite unreliable.

Robots, however, can be great at time sheets. (That's using the term "robots" pretty loosely here to include everything that falls under the AI umbrella.) Between machine learning, natural language processing, and predictive modeling, robots are already better than we are at tasks like filling in time sheets. That's why you need to get more comfortable with automation and everything else that is going to ~~take our jobs~~ make our jobs easier.

Here's What to Do

Don't worry, you don't have to be a tech prodigy to leverage automation in a positive way. The first step is to shift your mindset from a manual mindset to an automated mindset. This requires absolutely no technical skill. It just requires an ability to recognize how repetitive and predictable a task is. Let's take sales tasks as an example:

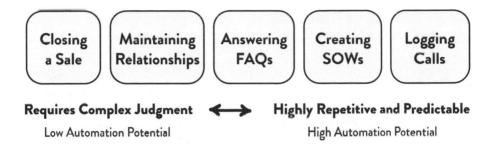

Requires Complex Judgment ⟷ **Highly Repetitive and Predictable**

Low Automation Potential   High Automation Potential

Now, that doesn't mean you actually *can* automate SOW generation or call logging immediately. In order to do that, you need the right people and the right tools. But, again, this step is just about seeing the potential. Once you see it, you can't unsee it. That's a great thing because it means you're able to be an automation advocate.

Once you've mastered step one, you can move on to the automation Venn diagram:

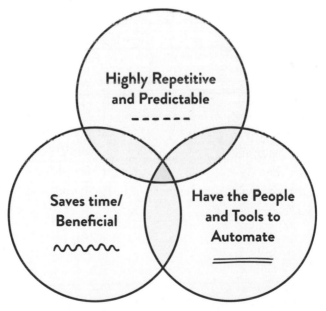

This Venn diagram will help you separate what theoretically *could* be automated from what can *actually* be automated. In order to automate a task or process, it needs to meet three criteria: It must be highly repetitive and predictable, it must save time and/or be highly beneficial, and you must have the people and tools needed to automate.

Let's talk a little more about that last one: the people and tools you need to automate processes and tasks. If your team or organization doesn't currently have those things, this is something for you to consider. Are there skill gaps that need to be filled? Are there entire roles that are missing? Are your systems ready for the future or are they clunky and antiquated? Can any software you already have perform some tasks you're not even aware of? These are the types of questions you'll ask once you're comfortable with automation. Keep asking and keep advocating.

Take Action

No one wants to waste their time on tasks that are brain-numbingly repetitive. They aren't a good use of your or your team's time, talent, or energy. Become an automation expert by shifting your mindset from a manual orientation to an automation orientation. Then work on building out the team members and tools you need to automate the right tasks.

36. Actually Use Your Data

Help People Feel: *Respected*

Harmful Habit: *Wasted Data and Time-Consuming Collection*

Successful Strategy: *Real Data Insights*

What's Gone Wrong

High-quality data has changed the world of sports, manufacturing, logistics—you name it. It saves time, allows new opportunities for objectivity, and can make predictions with stunning accuracy.

But here's the thing—for every amazing piece of game-changing data, there's something else that no one talks about: the absolute graveyard of data that never sees the light of day.

We've all seen it. Time sheets that get approved without being reviewed. Project timelines that never get analyzed. There's a staggering amount of wasted potential sitting somewhere in a hopelessly unaggregated or unvisualized state.

You know who's the most frustrated with this wasted potential? Your employees. They're the ones that have painstakingly collected all of that data. They were probably promised that this mountain of information was important for some reason no one can remember now.

It's completely demoralizing.

Here's What to Do

The good news is that the solution to this source of employee frustration has already been planned. Surely there was an original purpose to collecting the data you've asked employees to squirrel away (hint: If the reason is "it might be useful someday," you actually *haven't* identified a purpose).

Take some time to look at your data programs and your operational processes together. Evaluate the amount of effort needed to collect and process the data, and compare it with the potential outcomes. Rank each process on a scale from 1–10 in two areas:

1. **Difficulty of collecting and analyzing the data:** Think about this carefully, particularly the difficulty of analyzing the data. Do you have staff members who are qualified to analyze the data? Is your leadership team capable of interpreting the findings and translating that into real action? If not, the difficulty level may be higher than you think.

2. **Benefit of the actual output:** What, exactly, is there to gain by collecting and analyzing this data? Is it going to save significant time or money? Is it going to improve the quality of your products or services? The benefits should be clear and concise. They should also be *real*, not hypothetical.

Be brutally honest in your ratings. Once you're done, weigh the difficulty of collecting and analyzing the data against the benefit of the actual output. If your data collection practices are not worth it, cut them immediately. You will save countless person-hours and incalculable quantities of morale.

A final tip: Invite feedback when going through this process. Your people know how much work they've already been asked to put into data collection. Ask them what they think. Don't assume that your perspective is more valuable than theirs.

Take Action

Wasted data is not only a morale killer, but also a time killer. If you're not going to actually use your data, there's no point in collecting it. Carefully list and evaluate your data collection projects. Only keep those that are truly worth it.

37. Play Offense, Not Defense

Help People Feel: *Safe*
Harmful Habit: *Constant Reaction Mode*
Successful Strategy: *Proactive Focus on the Future*

What's Gone Wrong

Organizations can exist in different modes. In "offense" mode, the company is growing, creating new things, and radiating positive energy. When it's in "defense" mode, it's making cuts, hunting for problems that need to be stamped out, and running on stress and negative energy.

Businesses often want the results of offense mode but operate in defense mode. And then they are confused about why numbers aren't growing and people aren't thriving.

Let's make something clear: You want to be in offense mode. Defense mode is a survival state and almost never successfully turns itself around. It could even be the state before organization implosion. If you want to get out of it, then you have to stop making the same mistakes.

For example, if you want growth, you need to hire more people. Businesses get this wrong all the time. They cut positions and refuse to replace them until growth occurs. So the organization is attempting to function below the baseline, with an expectation of above-average results. In a situation like this, even staying at baseline performance is more than should be expected.

Here's What to Do

If your organization is currently stuck in the wrong mode and you want to turn things around, then you're going to have to start playing offense. There's no need to go overboard—no one is suggesting that your organization gets bloated. But you need to immediately start by ensuring that you are staffed and equipped for growth. Stop ignoring the gaping holes that you intend to fill "when you can." If you're not going to add staff, then reduce current priorities to fit the size of your team, make a realistic staffing plan that aligns with your goals, and stop squeezing the life out of everyone.

In general, go on the offensive and:

○ Invest money in hiring, systems, and resources.

○ Invest time in getting your organization into a healthy state.

○ Stop looking back at "what went wrong," and start looking forward to what you need now.

This also applies to culture, obviously. If your employee surveys show that people are stressed and frustrated, bringing down the hammer isn't going to help. Nurturing and fueling your people will. Defense mode will leave your people exhausted, overworked, and barely able to make their goals. If you keep treating them like that, it's never going to get better, no matter how many cheerful words you say.

Take Action

Making constant cuts and being on high alert for mistakes will strangle your business. You shouldn't expect to see positive growth if you're constantly making defensive moves. This mistake can also be a source of chronic stress, which can contribute to absenteeism, low productivity, and higher healthcare costs. Make sure you have the people and tools needed to achieve your goals. If you don't, put some of them on hold until you do. And if you really want to grow and thrive, go on the offensive and invest liberally.

38. Smash Bottlenecks (Including Your Own)

Help People Feel: *Valued*

Harmful Habit: *Hurry-Up-and-Wait Culture*

Successful Strategy: *Streamlined Processes*

What's Gone Wrong

Nothing is worse than hustling and hurrying to get something done, trying to make a deadline or satisfy a stakeholder, only to have everything come to a screeching halt. Roadblocks. Bottlenecks. Red tape. Sometimes it feels like you just can't get any momentum going.

Typically, the source of these bureaucratic nightmares is poor planning. Everyone is focused on getting work off their desk and onto someone else's. But they don't provide adequate time or resources for everything else that's happening along the way. That's how one person gets ten projects to review dumped on them the same day. Add in a dash of ego (from that manager that has to *personally* approve every single thing) and suddenly everything grinds to a halt in one or two trouble spots.

This all comes back to trust and autonomy. If you haven't built a team you can trust, it's difficult for operations to run smoothly.

Here's What to Do

You probably have so many little bottlenecks in your organization that it feels like "that's just the way it is." So take a step back and look for these two common types, then try the solutions with each.

The Ego Bottleneck

An ego bottleneck comes from a manager who has to be involved in *everything*. They have to personally see things and approve them, and if something isn't their idea, it is likely that they will interfere with lots of questions and pushback. As a result, the entire team—sometimes the entire company—revolves around them. At best, this person feels like they are adding important value, which may be partially true. At worst, they mainly just love the attention and feel like the organization exists to bring their ideas to life. Instead, be willing to delegate and listen. You hired your team because of their talent. Let them show you what they can do.

The Chaos Bottleneck

A chaos bottleneck happens as a result of poor planning. Everyone wants projects to go fast, but they don't leave time for all the steps that have to happen. Without enough planning, projects naturally hit sticking points. That might mean they need a certain person's skills, but that person wasn't notified in advance. Or that the boss wants to move on to the next step before the current step is done. No amount of sheer will can make the chaos go away. To address this type of bottleneck, you actually have to slow down and get organized instead. Plan the schedule carefully and share it with all stakeholders.

Both of these types of bottlenecks are frustrating and preventable. Your organization needs to be structured in a way that allows work to flow. When work is moving along at a manageable pace, everyone feels way more productive. Plus, employees can get more done and be more creative if they aren't constantly task switching. With more planning, they also have time to collaborate without feeling like they have to rush on to the next task.

Instead of thinking of bottlenecks as a hassle and just forcing people to deal with them, look at them as opportunities to make your organization run better. Plus, people will be happier if they don't have to constantly "hurry up and wait."

Take Action

Rushing to finish work only to have it sit on someone else's desk is such a buzz-kill. Unfortunately, a lot of employees feel that way all of the time. Either they're dealing with an ego-driven leader who forces their way into everything, or they don't have a solid enough schedule to prevent chaotic twists and turns. Step back, look at your bottlenecks, and break them down. If you're the cause, take steps to get yourself out of the way so that work can carry on more smoothly.

39. Start Over (Sometimes)

Help People Feel: *Valued*

Harmful Habit: *Old, Outdated Processes and Products*

Successful Strategy: *Simpler, Fresh Starts*

What's Gone Wrong

Fractured, chaotic businesses are unstable because they're always starting over. By contrast, stagnant, dinosaur businesses are unproductive because they *never* start over. They carry all of their baggage on their workers' backs, never acknowledging the drain all of that weight is causing. While you don't want to be impatient and wasteful, you also don't want to be obstinate and fossilized. The key is to find that sweet spot when hitting the rest button is just what the company needs.

In today's age, it is common to see an industry come to its knees in a three-to five-year period. A nimble start-up enters the scene, free of baggage and red tape, and creates a new way for customers to get what they want, often much more inexpensively and conveniently. While those new businesses may eventually also find themselves struggling for one reason or another, you can't deny that the original alacrity is exactly what people wanted.

If you're a well-established business, that doesn't mean that you have to throw everything away. But it does mean that you shouldn't be afraid to. Right now, you can probably think of a few processes or systems that are terribly overwrought and exhausting. Maintaining them is probably costing massive amounts of energy and time. Those are the areas to focus on.

We usually ignore these monoliths because they're overwhelming to even think about. It seems easier to just keep going. Sometimes that's because of the system itself, but other times it's because of the people who surround the system. "This is the way we've always done it" is bound to come up in a meeting on this topic. But if it is sucking the life out of your organization, it just isn't worth it. Be bold and start over with a fresh perspective.

Here's What to Do

Typically, these types of resets will take a medium amount of time and effort. If the process or product could be revamped overnight, someone would have already done it. But they aren't going to take years either. Typically, it will be something in the middle—more like a two- to twelve-month transition.

For example, let's say that you have a home-built tech system that you use for operations. Everyone knows that it is slow and clunky and that some parts of it are very unique to your business. Choosing a replacement will probably take about two months, then another two months to configure and implement, and, finally, two months to get everyone up and running in the new system. So you're looking at a six-month process. Which sounds like a lot until you realize that you should have done this five years ago. If you don't start now, you'll likely spend several more years dealing with the same frustrations. That's how you know it is time to start over.

Don't try to figure this out all by yourself. If you do, you'll end up with something that you *think* should work, but that absolutely doesn't. (Sound familiar?) Involve key stakeholders and those who use this system every day—they're going to have great perspective and ideas on what should be improved.

Take Action

We live in an age of reinvention—don't be afraid to partake! When you can, look at your most weighed-down, time-wasting systems, processes, or products, and start fresh. Go all the way back to the requirements, and work with your team to research, select, and implement something new. You'll all end up on fresher, firmer ground and better prepared for the future.

40. Reduce the Number of Stakeholders

Help People Feel: *Valued*

Harmful Habit: *Extraneous Unstructured Opinions*

Successful Strategy: *Simple, Clear Structure and Ownership*

What's Gone Wrong

Every overlap in your organization is also a potential gap. Because if both James and Gabriella get client feedback, but James thinks that Gabriella is going to get Client A feedback and Gabriella thinks the opposite, there's a decent chance that neither of them actually does it.

Decentralized organizations with limited hierarchy can be fantastic, but one major drawback is that the lack of structure can result in confusion and mess. Unless you rearrange your structure intentionally and thoughtfully, you end up with a lot of people investing themselves into situations that have little to do with them. Have you ever seen an accountant give feedback on what brand colors they like? Maybe they have great taste (or maybe not), but, even if they do, it's not a great use of anyone's time.

Even hierarchical businesses often have issues with overinflated structures that lead to a glut of stakeholders. How many people have to sign off on something before it can actually get done? This is where the law of triviality will kick in, and people (of all levels of expertise) will give a disproportionate amount of feedback to trivial issues instead of spending time on more meaningful (but complex) questions. Suddenly, you have a dozen executives fighting over a minor detail (google the "bicycle-shed effect" to learn more about this concept) that is a waste of everyone's time.

Here's What to Do

The solution to the too-many-stakeholders problem actually comes back to people having the authority to own their domain and your ability to trust that your team members are experts in their respective areas. Instead of having an amorphous team where everyone throws in their two cents, you want a structured, empowered team where each person brings solid experience to the table.

Let's go back to our example with James and Gabriella. Who are they and who is best suited to collect the necessary feedback? If James is the head of customer success and Gabriella is the head of sales, then perhaps they're both qualified in different ways. Specificity is key. James should get feedback on what customers find to be most useful, and Gabriella should find out what they are most interested in buying. That extra level of detail prevents them from stepping on each other's toes.

But what if Gabriella is actually the head of finance? Well, unless there are extraordinary circumstances at play, she shouldn't be a part of this process. If you involve everyone in every process, regardless of their actual expertise, then you'll be stuck in a productivity vortex. Sure, your head of finance should provide financial modeling or cost data. But they probably won't have experience with collecting feedback from customers. If not, get them out of the process. That way, everything can run more smoothly instead of constant interruption and second-guessing by extraneous players.

Take Action

Not all opinions are equal, nor does anyone have infinite time to wade through whose opinions are more valuable in a given situation. So, instead of allowing your processes and teams to bloat with extra people (and their opinions), keep it tight. Every person involved should be an informed team member with the right expertise for the job. They should know what is needed from them and be given time to adequately do the required work. Avoid bringing on "extra sets of eyes" who have no clear purpose, and don't allow uninformed outsiders to overload your processes.

chapter 6

Build a Welcoming Workplace Community

Modern businesses love to talk about diversity. They want all of the brownie points for saying the right things, so they gush on social media. But when it's time to enact real, tangible changes to how they do business? More often than not, there's silence.

Achieving real equity is one of the imperatives of our time. We know that there is a tremendous amount of work to be done to ensure that people of all races, genders, religions, ages, abilities, and backgrounds are represented and supported. It isn't going to happen without continuous effort. While businesses are happy to make big, glossy pledges, they aren't spending enough time on the real work that is going to make equity possible.

This chapter will cover several different areas of diversity, including some, like neurodiversity, that are not commonly discussed. The key to making progress in these areas lies on a strong foundation of respect for people's needs. Instead of ignoring them or expecting people to mold themselves to fit in, you must reshape your workplace so that inclusion is possible. That means changes big and small.

Each person on your team is unique. It's important that you understand their needs so that you can fully support them as individuals. The onus is on *you* to create a safe and welcoming workplace where each person's essential needs are met. In this chapter, you'll learn what to look out for, how to implement changes, and how to differentiate your own preferences from the needs of your team.

41. Know That Your Experience Is Not Universal

Help People Feel: *Safe*

Harmful Habit: *A Narrow Definition of What Is "Normal"*

Successful Strategy: *A Safe Space Where Everyone Is Recognized and Respected*

What's Gone Wrong

Our world has become hyper-personalized. Everything we eat, wear, watch, and do can be unique to us if we want it to be. You can get personalized show recommendations on your favorite streaming platform, food made exactly to your preferences, and shopping experiences based on your exact taste and buying history. While that's some cool innovation, it can also mean that it's easy to ignore any preferences other than your own.

You're the center of your universe. When you're in the middle of something, it's hard to see anything that's outside of your small sphere. It's hard to realize just how small your world might be in comparison with the many different lives others are living. Things you do, eat, wear, and say are very familiar to you but could be unfamiliar to someone else—and vice versa.

This is important to recognize as a leader. It's easy to think that your frame of reference is "normal." It's normal for you, isn't it? And that's fine. You just have to be careful not to assume that your experience is normal for others. The danger of that is discounting the very real experiences of others.

Here's What to Do

Identity is a layered concept. No one is just one thing. They're many, many things. All of those layers add up to make everyone a unique individual. Are there others that are similar to you? Absolutely. But there are many, many more people who are different from you.

Here are some categories that make up our identities:

- Race
- Age
- Gender Identity
- Level of Income
- Religion
- Native Language

- Sexual Orientation
- Places You've Lived
- Level of Education
- Occupation
- Health Conditions
- Physical and Mental Abilities

In general, the corporate world is doing a somewhat better job talking about topics like race and ableism. However, it still isn't really talking about intersectionality. Kimberlé W. Crenshaw, JD, first coined the term "intersectionality" in 1989. It is the study of overlapping or intersecting social identities and related systems of oppression, domination, or discrimination. It is important that leaders understand that identity is complex and multilayered.

Diverse perspectives and experiences are invaluable. Remind yourself that the way you experience the world is different from what others experience so that you're careful not to make incorrect and unfair assumptions. For example, you may feel perfectly safe in your day-to-day life or that household goods are easily affordable—but that doesn't mean that everyone does.

Why does it matter to think about how people are unique? Because you, as a leader, have a lot of influence on those around you. If people who aren't like you are being forced to fit into your world, how can they expect to feel welcome?

Take Action

Our world is changing in positive ways that allow people more space to be themselves. That's good for everyone. It also means that the concept of "normality" might actually be more harmful than it is helpful. Remember, your experience and identity are influenced by many factors that make you unique. Just be careful not to assume that others' experiences are just like yours. As a leader, it's important that you are welcoming of all members of your team.

42. Accommodate Enthusiastically

Help People Feel: *Safe*

Harmful Habit: *Inflexible "One-Size-Fits-All" Accommodations*

Successful Strategy: *Flexible Options*

What's Gone Wrong

It's time to start thinking about accommodations differently. Right now, when employees need accommodations, they usually only ask for them as a last resort. They're terrified to be viewed as needy, and they're often scared that they'll be met with suspicion, annoyed sighs, and "no"s. Leaders should start thinking about the workplace as less of a prix fixe menu and more like a build-your-own bar.

For a long time, businesses have attempted to force everyone into a homogenized approach, meaning that everyone of the same status gets the same treatment and the same stuff. They did this because they wanted the appearance of fairness (actual fairness is debatable). What happened? A huge amount of emphasis was placed on status as the only way to earn "more." As we all know, equality doesn't equal equity. In fact, giving everyone the same thing often causes or exacerbates *in*equity. What happens when someone with a dairy allergy visits a restaurant that forbids substitutions? They leave hungry and annoyed. You certainly don't want your staff to feel the same way.

Here's What to Do

Now, what happens when that same dairy-intolerant individual visits a restaurant with a flexible menu? They get what they want. Nothing is forced on them. Instead, they get to look at all of the options and choose what works best for them.

Businesses that adopt a build-your-own approach early on will have a huge competitive advantage. They'll stop wasting resources that employees are being given that they don't want and/or can't use. And their employees will be happier with what they actually get. Take a look at these differences:

	Prix Fixe Approach	Build-Your-Own Approach
Workspace	All employees of the same status are given the same desk, equipment, etc. in a one-size-fits-all approach.	Employees are allowed to choose from available workspaces and may select their own equipment from a predetermined set of options.
Schedule	All employees must work the same hours.	Employees are allowed to set their own schedules as long as they complete their job requirements.
Rewards	All employees are given the same rewards.	Employees are allowed to choose the type of reward or specific reward item they prefer.

This doesn't have to be an expansion of resources. It can simply be a different approach that better fits everyone's needs.

Take Action

Instead of assuming that everyone is the same, try assuming that everyone is different. By allowing people to choose from a menu of preapproved options, you allow them to get what they want without straining your budget or causing "unfairness." Making this approach your new default benefits everyone and will likely leave employees feeling happier because their personal needs are being better addressed.

43. Stop Pretending You Don't See Color

Help People Feel: *Safe*

Harmful Habit: *Lying about Being "Colorblind"*

Successful Strategy: *Honest Conversations about Race*

What's Gone Wrong

Let's say that sometime, long ago, there were good intentions that led someone to say, "I don't see color." The idea that you would want to judge someone purely on their accomplishments and not on their race is alluring. But it's also dangerously naive because it's impossible to do. There are two main problems with pretending you don't see color:

1. **You ignore your own biases.** Every interaction you witness and every image you see is layered with context clues that tell you what to think and feel about someone. Those are biases. We all want to believe that we're good people who do the right thing in a given moment. If you want that to be true, it's important to recognize and evaluate your own biases (we all have them).
2. **You make equity impossible.** When you pretend you don't see color, you ignore all of the challenges people face. It's your job as a leader and a human to recognize when a setup isn't fair and to keep making changes until they are.

Here's What to Do

A positive workplace is one that is just, fair, and equitable. Here's how to get there.

Step 1: Educate Yourself on Bias and Inequity

There are some inequities that you know about, but there are probably many, many more that you don't. Do you know what the school-to-prison pipeline is? How about the long-term financial effects of redlining? Elements of racism and bias are present in almost every corporate structure and system imaginable, even if you think your business doesn't "relate" to race. Make learning about biases, inequities, and issues a serious part of your job, and be sure to proactively seek out continuing education.

Step 2: Get Comfortable Talking about Race

It's rude and taboo to talk about race, right? Wrong. This is a myth that has been perpetuated to keep the status quo in place—namely, to keep the powerful (read: white people) in power. This is a difficult change to make because it's very deeply ingrained. In fact, one of the reasons people like to pretend they "don't see color" is to avoid difficult conversations.

You probably don't have a lot of experience talking about race, so you're going to need to practice. Get reputable advice on how to do it correctly. Watch out for euphemistic language (don't say "urban" if you mean "Black"). Speak clearly and plainly. Be willing to make some mistakes (and apologize for them). Otherwise, you aren't really saying anything at all.

Step 3: Pick Up the Mantle

All of this enlightenment is meaningless if it isn't backed up with real action. You should dedicate time to specific projects that achieve real results. People are tired of all of the talk that leads to nothing. Pick up that mantle and take it seriously.

Where should you start? Everyone is different, but it's best to start with your area of expertise. What is under your specific purview? Is it hiring? Budget? Learning programs? Control what you can and be an advocate everywhere else.

Take Action

"I don't see color" is an offensive statement. It ignores the very real challenges that People of Color face every day. A positive workplace is one that is comfortable and equitable. Take that responsibility seriously by educating yourself, speaking plainly, and consciously taking action to advance racial justice.

44. Take Inclusion and Representation Seriously

Help People Feel: *Safe*

Harmful Habit: *Teams or Organizations Disproportionately Dominated by White, Male, Cis, Able People*

Successful Strategy: *Fair Representation at All Levels of the Organization*

What's Gone Wrong

In order to have a positive workplace culture and high "employee engagement," your company has to address inclusion. Inclusion is making sure that everyone has a seat at the table and that their ideas and perspectives are valued.

Here's What to Do

You're not going to wake up one day to find that inclusion has been achieved without any action from you. If you're thinking "there's nothing I can do," you're wrong. It is your responsibility to achieve inclusion as it pertains to your purview. Do you run a team? If so, is your team makeup diverse? Look at your team's compensation levels and be sure you don't need to make any adjustments (see #12: Check the Scoreboard for Inequitable Pay in Chapter 3). What about the work you produce? Does it include and serve people across demographics?

Be Informed

The key to inclusion is understanding who's missing from the table. In order to do that, you need some representative data. There are a few ways to slice and dice it. You might want to base your data pool on the entire adult population, the demographics of your customer base, or global data. Here are some recent numbers representing the US adult population:

- Possible Source 1: www.hubspot.com/diversity/report
- Possible Source 2: https://news.linkedin.com/2021/october/2021-workforce-diversity-report

This data should serve as a benchmark across all levels of your organization. For example, if the data shows that 7.5 percent of the population is Hispanic, but your leadership is only 1 percent Hispanic, you have a problem. Unless you're one of a handful of companies, you probably haven't achieved that yet.

Show Your Work

No matter what type of work you do, inclusion should be a fundamental consideration. You also need it in the work you actually produce. Here are some examples of what that might be like in different industries or functions:

- **Marketing firm:** Casting diverse groups of models for campaigns
- **Healthcare:** Providers are informed on care for diverse patient populations
- **Education:** Financial aid and scholarships are accessible to all
- **Beauty:** Products are widely available for all skin colors, hair textures, and body types
- **Architecture:** Spaces are accessible for all levels of ability and gender identities

Every industry and job function is different. The important thing is to recognize where you stand and try to keep improving.

Expand Your Pipeline

Finally, it's time to address changing your hiring practices. How are you advertising open positions? Where do you recruit? Are your interview teams inclusive? Pick one task you can do now and get started. For example, ensuring that all interview teams are equally composed of men and women is a simple, straightforward change that can make a big difference.

When you're able to go one step further, work on ways to grow an inclusive talent pipeline even more. This might mean becoming a mentor for students or offering apprentice programs. Branch out as wide as you can.

Take Action

Inclusion and representation are everyone's responsibility, including you. Take this task seriously and commit to real action. This means educating yourself by examining reputable diversity data, ensuring your work is inclusive, and changing your hiring and outreach programs to diversify your talent pipeline.

45. Create Safety for All Genders

Help People Feel: *Safe*

Harmful Habit: *Gender Bias*

Successful Strategy: *Secure, Inclusive Spaces*

What's Gone Wrong

The world can be a dangerous place. Work shouldn't have to be—but it is for many people.

Pause and think about that for a moment. Do you want anyone to feel fundamentally unsafe in your workplace? If there were visible physical hazards, like a broken step, would you fix them? Of course you would. If those hazards are obvious to some people but not to others, they are still as crucial to fix.

Our collective understanding of the gender spectrum is evolving. While biological sex has always been more diverse than the male/female designations, it is such a taboo topic that most people have learned very little about it.

Even if your organization seeks to be progressively inclusive, "work" is still one of the most rigid social structures. Think about how harshly a cisgender person is judged for wearing the "wrong" thing in a corporate setting. Wardrobe doesn't have anything to do with job performance, but many people are adamant that "professional dress" is essential. For a gender non conforming person, this can be especially difficult. They should be able to dress in a way that is comfortable for them without fear of being insulted, disrespected, or disregarded.

Here's What to Do

To start, you can't ignore the issue of gender identity. Similar to pretending you don't see color, you can't pretend not to see gender. It affects everything we do and see. Instead, dedicate yourself to understanding and advancing gender inclusivity.

Once you understand the lay of the land, you'll be better prepared to ensure safety and inclusion for everyone on the gender spectrum.

You can't just snap your fingers and change the world overnight. But you can start building more safety right now. Here are some actions to get you started:

○ **Create physical safety:** Ensure that any physical spaces your business uses are inclusive and safe. That includes private areas, like bathrooms and offices, and surrounding areas, like parking lots and hallways, which should be well lit and secure.

○ **Use inclusive language:** Many of us grew up with phrases like "guys" that seemed harmless and normal. Switch to simple, inclusive phrases like "everyone" instead.

○ **Share your pronouns:** When you share your pronoun preferences, you normalize it for others. You can also ask people what pronouns they prefer instead of assuming.

○ **Default to "they":** Forget what your schoolteacher told you about pronouns. Language authorities like Merriam-Webster and the MLA and APA now endorse using "they" as a default singular pronoun.

○ **Involve all genders in decision-making:** You don't know what you don't know. So involve all perspectives and solicit outside help if you need it.

○ **Make your stance known:** It doesn't help anyone if you secretly support gender diversity. Make your support well known so that people know that you and your team are safe.

None of these actions alone is enough to make a difference. But, together, they do shift things in the right direction. It's worth the minimal effort involved to make people feel more secure and welcome.

Take Action

All people should feel safe and welcome at work. Unfortunately, that is not the case for everyone, especially people who do not identify as part of the old-fashioned gender binary. As a leader, you should push for changes in your workplace to make it more gender inclusive. The changes you make help to make the workplace more hospitable for others.

46. Support Different Learning Styles

Help People Feel: *Respected*

Harmful Habit: *Poor or Standardized Teaching Techniques*

Successful Strategy: *Diverse Teaching Strategies and Styles*

What's Gone Wrong

Good leaders are good teachers. In fact, teaching is a core leadership skill that is often overlooked in favor of tired old clichés like *strategy* and *efficiency*. Many leaders are never taught any adult education techniques. They tend to get by on simply sharing what they know. But a leader with strong teaching skills is unstoppable—and their employees will feel that they don't just have a boss, they have someone who's invested in their growth and development.

Teaching is remarkably complex. Any parent who has seen their child go through a modern curriculum knows that the old repetition-based methods that were once popular are long gone. Yes, that change means that you need to learn some new techniques. But it also means that there are a wide variety of styles and strategies to help you up your teaching game.

Everyone learns differently. Understanding different learning needs and combining them effectively will help your team members connect and grow. Remember, people want to learn. But if you approach them in a way that is unmotivating or unappealing, it's likely that they won't engage with or remember your teachings.

Here's What to Do

If you're teaching a group, it's best to incorporate a range of styles so that everyone's needs are supported. This isn't just for formal learning situations—you should be intentional any time you're trying to impart information. For example, when you're rolling out a new initiative or even trying to solve a new problem, these techniques can be invaluable.

The VARK model is a popular set of learning styles that was defined by Neil D. Fleming and Colleen Mills. It stands for visual, auditory, reading/writing, and kinesthetic.

- **V**isual: Visual learners need to see something to understand it. They benefit from images, charts, and demonstrations.

- **A**uditory: Auditory learners benefit from listening and discussing. They often enjoy podcasts, audiobooks, and videos that have an audio component.

- **R**eading/Writing: Learners that prefer reading and writing benefit from time to read independently, note-taking, and writing about what they've learned.

- **K**inesthetic: Kinesthetic learners are tactile and will often say, "I'll get it when I'm able to do it." They benefit from hands-on activities and practical approaches.

Variety and integration are key. You probably won't be able to include every style in all of your activities, but keep trying. You may notice that your team gravitates toward one or two styles. Ask them for feedback so they can tell you what's working and what's not.

Take Action

As a leader, you have so much to share. If you're not thinking about different learning styles, your people probably aren't paying very close attention to your teachings. Adult learners are busy and learn in different ways. Help them better understand what you're sharing by mixing modalities from the VARK model, and pursue continuing education to help make you a better teacher.

47. Build Cognitive Diversity

Help People Feel: *Respected*

Harmful Habit: *Intolerance for Different Cognitive Abilities*

Successful Strategy: *Respect and Inclusion*

What's Gone Wrong

Cognitive diversity means including people with a wide variety of thinking styles, problem-solving abilities, and mental perspectives. Many talented, knowledgeable potential workers have conditions like ADHD, dyslexia, dyspraxia, or are on the autism spectrum.

Cognitive diversity is an area that hasn't been as widely discussed in our modern lexicon as some other diversity, equity, and inclusion topics. In fact, cognitive abilities and problem-solving styles are often viewed as a hierarchy, with "normal" styles at the top and everything else at the bottom. Even when we're measuring more objectively (in a cognitive test, for example), abilities are outright ignored if a person's outward presentation is atypical.

For example, common abilities for individuals on the autism spectrum include impressive knowledge in specific areas of interest. However, if that individual doesn't articulate their knowledge in a neurotypical way, their expertise is viewed as less important. Think about it objectively for a moment. Not all jobs require neurotypical presentation. And continuing to exclude people with different cognitive characteristics perpetuates the idea that there is no room in business for anyone whose style is different than what we've been told is normal. But there is. It's the right thing to do, and it *ultimately* benefits the business.

Here's What to Do

First, you need to address the interview process. Traditional interviews heavily favor neurotypical individuals. Some interview software even measures things like eye contact and speech pattern and ranks candidates on their performance. It's basically a high-tech way to completely weed out everyone who isn't neurotypical.

Truthfully, human judgment isn't much better. We've been taught to negatively judge any form of neurodivergent communication and look past true abilities in favor of their ability to conform. So proactive education is necessary. Teach your staff to focus on the unique requirements for each job. Instead of weeding out anyone who is different, focus on the specific skills and abilities a role needs. If someone is great with numbers and can help you implement new financial systems, you can support them if they require a quiet work environment. Allow for more flexibility and open-mindedness.

Once they are placed in a role, you will need to empower neurodivergent workers as they encounter the judgments of others. If the person has said they would like your help, you can step in and be an ally. But don't assume that's the case. If they're doing well at their job but they work in unique ways, don't let anyone devalue their contributions. Don't try to force them to fit the corporate mold. It's unnecessary and unfair. Instead, make it clear that your working environment will welcome people to work in different ways. That may mean alternative schedules or clear, formal methods for new work requests. Those are perfectly reasonable accommodations that ultimately benefit everyone involved.

Finally, a warning to keep in mind: Neurodiverse abilities may be so beneficial that you should stop and ask yourself: Are this person's skills being exploited? If you have a star who everyone turns to for statistical analysis, consider the burden that employee is being forced to carry. Are you ensuring that people will be generously compensated for their abilities? Are you informed about what they need in order to thrive? Are there systems in place to fully support their needs?

Take Action

Cognitive diversity is a developing area. Embrace cognitive diversity and make room for more thinking and problem-solving styles within your organization. Actively fight bias in the interviewing process, and then offer support to workers once they are placed in their roles. Lead the way in opening your organization up and making a more welcoming workplace.

48. Stop Centering Heteronormativity

Help People Feel: *Safe*

Harmful Habit: *Old-Fashioned Assumptions and Norms*

Successful Strategy: *A Welcoming but Noninvasive Workplace*

What's Gone Wrong

It's time for the corporate world to come out of the proverbial closet. Despite the progress that the LGBTQIA+ community has made, the corporate world is still largely hiding from it. Businesses are putting on an inclusive front, but in the boardroom it's business as usual.

Centering heteronormativity is something that heterosexual people often do without even realizing it. "What does your wife do?" Samantha asks her new colleague Brad. She noticed his wedding ring and made an incorrect assumption. The awkward moment that follows is deafening.

But this goes beyond someone putting their foot in their mouth. Much of the world is not very safe or comfortable for LGBTQIA+ people. The workplace is deeply entrenched in social structures that do not welcome change or nonconformity. The overwhelming message is that you have to fit in if you want to be successful, which means that accessing success is based on your ability to integrate into these existing structures. Everything, from professional dress to valued characteristics, is based on a heteronormative culture dominated by men. The further you are from being a cis, white, heterosexual man, the more difficult it will be to climb the corporate ladder.

Changing the shape of power structures takes effort. It doesn't happen on its own. Your small and large changes can make quite a difference.

Here's What to Do

Decentering heteronormativity is the solution here. Imagine a bull's-eye shape with heteronormative people in the center and others further out, depending on how much "different" they are viewed as being. The structure has absolutely nothing to do with talent or ability. But it does have everything to do with who's an insider and who's an outsider. What would happen if you moved the center of the bull's-eye? Suddenly power could be more accessible to people who weren't at the center before. Even better, what if the whole structure morphed into a ball? If that happened, then everyone could be equally close to the center.

The key is to stop making assumptions. Even if heterosexual relationships are what you're used to, you need to remember that there are many different kinds of relationships and families. Instead of assuming that everyone is the same, you're better off assuming that everyone is different.

Further, everyone is going to have different levels of comfort with what they want to share about themselves at work. Your job is to help people feel welcome and safe, which includes respecting their privacy. Never ask invasive questions—people will share if they want to.

In addition to being careful not to make assumptions about who is heterosexual, don't assume that anyone is homosexual, bisexual, or any other orientation. It's true that some outward characteristics have been adopted by different communities to signal within those communities. That wasn't necessarily done for style—it was for safety. So don't disrupt that safety by invasively guessing what their clothing, hairstyle, etc. might "mean." Again, if someone wants you to know, they will tell you.

Take Action

Most of the corporate world continues to keep their doors tightly closed to anyone that is "different," especially members of LGBTQIA+ communities. Many talented professionals have either been excluded or felt unwelcome. If you help your company stop centering heteronormativity and instead assume that each person is unique, you can create a much more level playing field that is accessible to all.

49. Make Space for All Levels of Physical Ability

Help People Feel: *Safe*

Harmful Habit: *Workplaces That Do Not Actively Welcome People with a Disability*

Successful Strategy: *Personalized Spaces That Are Safe and Welcoming*

What's Gone Wrong

When it comes to accessibility, most businesses seem to think that all they have to do is comply with the Americans with Disabilities Act and call it a day. That's following the rules, right? But there's a big difference between doing what you *have* to do and doing *everything* you can do.

According to the Centers for Disease Control and Prevention, one in four Americans lives with some form of disability. But you certainly don't see that represented in the workplace. We've done very little to make space for people with different levels of ability. As a result, they haven't been able to access many types of jobs. Sadly, many organizations seem to take an "out of sight, out of mind" approach to this issue.

Here's What to Do

When it comes to making space for all abilities, start with the actual, physical space. Some changes can be simple. Most aren't going to cost a lot of money; they are just more personalized so that all types of people can work comfortably. Options are key. You can:

- Offer the option to work remotely full time.
- Let people choose their own office furniture and setup.

- Provide diverse equipment to meet different needs.
- Use technology liberally and be aware of new tech that may improve workplace accessibility.

There's also the nonphysical space to consider. You may need to make some of the ways of working more accessible. You can:

- Ask for frequent feedback (and actually do something about it).
- Ensure that the environment is welcoming, patient, and respectful.
- Give people with different abilities options for coaching, assistance, or support.
- Don't base promotions and hiring on only "traditional" markers for success.
- Be aware of different physical and mental disabilities so that you know how to help.
- Prioritize health and safety above all else.

As you can see, these are relatively basic ideas. It doesn't take much to make your workplace accessible and hospitable. You just need to work on your mindset and ditch the one-size-fits-all approach.

Take Action

We are not doing enough to create safe space in the workplace for people with disabilities. Yes, you need to know and follow all of the ADA requirements that apply to your space. But there is much more that you can do, mostly by taking a flexible, personalized approach.

50. Revisit Your Holiday Calendar

Help People Feel: *Respected*

Harmful Habit: *Inflexible, Standard Holiday Calendars*

Successful Strategy: *Flexible Holiday Options*

What's Gone Wrong

How many paid holidays does your organization offer? Out of those that are fixed (not floating), how many are affiliated with a religion? If you're following the US federal holidays, then the only religious holiday represented on the list is Christmas.

You may think, "It's only one day, what's the big deal?" Calm down, there's no war on Christmas here. The problem isn't in giving that one day off, but in what you're *not* giving. There may be more you can do to respect people's diverse religious backgrounds.

Recently, some brilliant content creators on social media have been showing what it's like to "flip the script" on holiday schedules. Meaning, instead of considering Christian holidays to be the "normal" holidays, showing what it would be like if other religions were the most prominent in our culture.

Christianity still has a major stronghold in America, but that doesn't make non-Christian events any less important. There's no need to diminish any celebrations you currently have—but you can be more open and courteous to other options as well.

Here's What to Do

Planning ahead and offering flexible options will do a lot to help people feel more comfortable with their holiday observances. If you don't, that leaves people to beg for each individual holiday—*every year*.

Asking for time off for religious or cultural holidays can put people into awkward and uncomfortable situations. No one should have to justify their religious practices or feel like they have to ask a favor of their boss in order to celebrate them. It isn't their job to educate you about their culture. Nor is it your place to decide whether a holiday is "real" or "important."

So instead of backing yourself into a corner, proactively offer floating holiday options. You can still have your core holidays (which should be in addition to your other paid time off). It would be appropriate to offer two to four floating holidays for employees to use. And they should have full control over when they get to use them. They should never be made to feel guilty because their holiday falls on a "bad day." Avoid those situations by knowing when your team members intend to take their floating holidays, and then being sure not to schedule major events for those days. That way, there never have to be any conflicts. It also helps to allow people to use this holiday time over multiple and/or consecutive days, which they may want to use for holidays like Ramadan or Passover, which are celebrated over multiple days.

What about employees who have no religious affiliation? Should they miss out? Certainly not. Work with them. Even if they aren't religious, there may be important cultural days like Lunar New Year or certain countries' independence days that they would like to honor. If not, simply allow them to use the days as they wish.

Take Action

No one culture should be more important or more celebrated than any other in the workplace. Many non-Christian people find themselves having to explain their holidays over and over again to bosses who are unfamiliar so that they can try to get time off to observe. Offering flexible floating holidays makes things more equitable and allows you to plan ahead so employees can truly enjoy that holiday time.

chapter 7

Cultivate a Healthy Work-Life Balance

Work is part of life. For some, it can be a path to fulfillment, pursuant to meaningful goals. For others, it can be a means to an end, allowing them to access the lifestyle they want. Or it can be both. Either way, it's important to keep perspective—work should only be *part* of your life.

Work-life balance is a much-discussed topic. For some, it can even be a bit triggering if they've dedicated so much of their life to work that the whole concept feels alien and uncomfortable.

Hard work is one of the cornerstones of society. There's almost nothing worse you could call someone than lazy. But work-life balance doesn't have anything to do with laziness. It has everything to do with leading a satisfying life where people have time for things outside of work that matter to them.

Your role in improving employee work-life balance will depend on your position. If you have the ability to make and enforce company-wide policies, then you can make more concrete changes like increasing total PTO days. Even if you don't, however, you can still be a strong influence on the people around you.

A huge determining factor in work-life balance is the company's overall attitude to time outside of work. If every moment away from work is treated with hostility, it makes people feel extremely uncomfortable. There's no reason to make people feel guilty for having a life. This chapter will focus on practicing this and other ways you can improve work-life balance for your team (and for yourself too).

51. Make Time Off Sacrosanct

Help People Feel: *Valued*

Harmful Habit: *Looking Down On or Judging Time Off*

Successful Strategy: *Relaxing, Undistracted Time Off*

What's Gone Wrong

There are three types of workers that go on vacation. There's Bob, who's somehow emailing you back right away from the Maldives. There's Cameron, who checks their email twice a day "just so things don't pile up." And there's Veronica, who isn't answering your call unless there's a real emergency.

Corporations tend to *love* Bob. Bob's getting a little plaque to sit on his desk for outstanding dedication to the company. They're tolerant of Cameron. Unfortunately, many companies think Veronica is lazy and/or selfish. When it came time for annual raises, executives were so thrilled with Bob that he got a raise that was double Veronica's.

Is it worth it? Is it necessary to push ourselves as hard as humanly possible with absolutely no breaks? No, it is not. It's actually just terribly sad. And exhausting. And unhealthy.

Breaks are necessary for rest and recuperation. They also spur creativity and give a fresh perspective that tends to improve your work when you return. It's in everyone's best interest that workers take liberal amounts of time off. Unfortunately, the mindset of not taking much time off has become deeply ingrained in US culture. To upend it, you need to do more than just taking your PTO and encouraging others to do the same. In order to reset, you need to take proactive and systemic action.

Here's What to Do

Systemic problems need systemic solutions. Here are four steps you can continuously take to make time off truly nonnegotiable:

1. **Set PTO minimums:** After the failure that was the "unlimited PTO" wave, encouraging people to take their PTO is going to require a firmer push. Try setting PTO minimums. Be liberal with the number of days required—being stingy will only perpetuate the idea that fewer is better.

2. **Staff accordingly:** This is where most organizations' PTO planning and policies fail. They have no systemic solution for who is going to do the work when people take their PTO. This makes people afraid to take it, and it also forces them to pick up the slack when others do. The solution isn't complicated: Hire more people.

3. **Set a positive example:** This is the fun part. Take *your* PTO. It's extremely common to hear executives or HR professionals espouse the benefits of taking PTO and then fail to actually take it themselves. That sends the message that the Bobs of the world are still going to be preferred. It's a sadistic game and, again, it's not worth it. Lead by example.

4. **Check on your skeptics:** If you've taken steps 1–3 seriously, you should be in good shape. But, as with any change of management process, you're going to have resisters. They're going to hold out as long as possible. And they're going to judge the people who *are* taking their time off. Don't pressure these people, just talk with them. Ask them if they want scheduled time off throughout the year or if they plan to take it all at the end. Make sure they know that either plan is okay with you but that time off is an important part of the company's values.

Take Action

Companies often say that they want people to take time off...but employees don't believe them. That's because companies keep rewarding people who *don't* take their time off, which tells them that what their leaders *really* want is for them to work themselves into oblivion with no breaks. In order to make people comfortable enough to change their behavior, you need to show and model for them that the company truly does value PTO. Don't deprive yourself or others of the joy of rest and relaxation.

52. Set Working Hours (and Stick to Them)

Help People Feel: *Respected*

Harmful Habit: *Expectations of 24/7 Availability*

Successful Strategy: *Reasonable Working Hours*

What's Gone Wrong

Want to know a surefire way to give your employees a heart attack and ruin their night of sleep? Send them an email at 11 p.m. that says, "Hey, can we meet first thing in the morning?" and nothing else. That way, they'll have nightmares about getting fired all night (that is, if they sleep at all).

Cell phones are great. Having the Internet in our pockets has brought us endless joy and access to unlimited information and communication. But you know what *isn't* great? Getting work messages at all hours of the day and night.

Since the dawn of the BlackBerry, we've been trying to figure out how to resist the temptation of immediately reading and responding to every work message. That's more than twenty years of perpetual exhaustion and anxiety.

Many leaders' days are extremely full—in fact, it's common to see leaders who are fully booked with back-to-back meetings during the "normal" workday. When do they do actual work and respond to messages? After hours. Sometimes that is right after work or in the early morning, but *most* often it's late at night. After dinner, after bedtime, after the world quiets down and it's possible to find some time to *think*.

Clearly there are many unhealthy red flags here to address—for now, we'll just tackle what you can do as a leader to limit communications to appropriate business hours.

Here's What to Do

If communicating during off-hours works for you, that's fine. The key is using a handy-dandy tool that allows you to work when you want *and* respects your employees' downtime: the delay feature.

Gmail, Outlook, and other major email providers all have features that allow you to delay sending or to schedule your emails. It's remarkably simple. Spend a few minutes figuring out how your system works, then start using it when you send messages off-hours.

Set a strict communications cutoff at the end of your company's workday. If there isn't an emergency (a real one; see #68: Shut Down Fake Emergencies in Chapter 8), then delay all of your emails so that they don't send until the next morning. You don't want your employees worrying about regular tasks in the evenings; that's their time to recharge for the next day.

Once you've established this rule for yourself, suggest it to everyone else on your team. Anyone can make this small change and it benefits the entire group. Explain why you want to quiet the off-hours noise and make sure everyone knows how to use the features correctly. If your team is spread out across time zones, discuss working hours as a group and set rules that work for everyone.

If it's within your sphere of influence, you can even try to take the communications cutoff a step further by working with IT to set times when emails can and can't be sent. It will take a bit of extra planning (and can be tricky if your company is global), but it will also solidify the practice you're requesting.

Take Action

Workaholics often work at all hours of the day. It's one thing when they do, but it's another when they suck others into their stressed-out, always-on state. Use your power as a team leader to set a clear communications cutoff and use the delay feature for nonurgent emails that are written off-hours. Even then, don't overdo it or your employees will end up with a full inbox at 8 a.m. Once you've adopted this behavior for yourself, speak to your team and teach them how to do the same.

53. Be Realistic about "Above and Beyond"

Help People Feel: *Valued*

Harmful Habit: *Unrealistic Expectations about Dedication and Work-Life Balance*

Successful Strategy: *A Standard of Good Performance at a Normal, Realistic Number of Hours*

What's Gone Wrong

How do you rate the work of someone who works hard all year long? Who takes initiative and makes sure their projects are done on time, even when they have to work extra hours? Someone who doesn't give up when they meet obstacles? If you're like most corporations, the answer is probably "Meets Expectations." And they're rated a three on a five-point scale.

Corporations are greedy for people's time. Since most employees have become salaried, too many companies feel entitled to as much of your time as they want. The more, the better. For this reason, they promote an unyielding "hustle culture," where "above and beyond" is the expectation and anything else is considered lazy and insufficient.

Ironically, they don't extend the same effort in return. They don't give "above and beyond" compensation or recognition. They act like you're lucky to even be thanked. This pressure can be particularly difficult for people who grew up with cultural pressure to perform (research the "model minority" myth for more information).

This tension came to a head in 2022 when, after years of over-the-top effort in extraordinary circumstances, businesses continued to ask for energy that employees simply didn't have. This brought about the infamous "quiet quitting" movement, leading to a generational brawl over what it meant to adequately perform a job.

Here's What to Do

It's time for businesses to reset their expectations. It is unrealistic to ask people to perform at an eleven every day of the year. "Above and beyond" should be saved for extraordinary circumstances. Let's say that you are working on an important product launch. It might be necessary to put in extra effort for 2–3 weeks prior to the launch. Launch day is probably going to be a very big day. But anything longer than three weeks isn't realistic. Don't try to ask people to exhaust themselves for a month or more—they'll just end up burning out and quitting.

Similarly, if you're going to allow employees to really hustle during special circumstances (which should be no more than 2–3 times per year), then you should also ensure that there will be lulls. A lull is a time when it's okay to relax a bit more and take a little more time to recharge. In some industries, lulls are seasonal. There might be times when consumers or production are less active. There's no point in expecting immense effort during a lull. In fact, it's the perfect time to back off a little.

And remember, your business is not the center of the universe. Sometimes an employee may need to ease up for personal reasons, like taking care of a family member or basic mental health. That doesn't mean you should immediately demote them down to part-time (unless that's what they want). Instead, recognize the natural cycles people go through and allow space for temperance in addition to times of intensity.

Finally, "above and beyond" effort must be met with "above and beyond" rewards. If someone is able to overdeliver 2–3 times per year, you should recognize that effort as exceeding expectations. Rate it accordingly and give them a raise that is significantly more than what is typical.

Take Action

Constant expectations of "above and beyond" effort is predatory. We are now long past the point where this is acceptable. You can realistically hope that an employee can offer extraordinary effort when there are extraordinary circumstances to match (and a reward should follow). If that happens, you should also allow for lulls.

54. Provide Opportunities for Remote Work

Help People Feel: *Respected*

Harmful Habit: *Obsession with Going Back to the Office*

Successful Strategy: *Investing in Dispersed Teams*

What's Gone Wrong

Before the pandemic, research like a 2013 study of 16,000 employees at Ctrip had already shown that workers were more productive at home than in an office. There are myriad reasons for this, including less commute time, fewer distractions, more personalized environments, and greater freedom.

Workers also want flexibility to make their own choices. During the pandemic, many had a chance to see what it was like not to spend forty hours a week under a drop ceiling. And they liked it.

That's why the majority of workers now prefer to have the option to work from home as much as they want. There's one noticeable group of holdouts: executives.

Executives are lagging behind this trend, and some of them are even renewing leases on office space that will likely never be fully occupied again. Some ego-driven leaders probably miss the power and control that came with being able to see their workers all day, every day, while others misguidedly feel like the only way to ensure good team relations is to have everyone under one roof.

Here's What to Do

Instead of resisting change, acknowledge that remote work is here to stay. Focus on mitigating the challenges that come with remote work and offering real, flexible options that meet your team's needs.

First:

Work with each person on your team to help them settle into their desired work arrangement. It's important to reserve some budget for this. Many companies are offering yearly stipends for ergonomic home office setups (something they would have sponsored in a central office anyway). If your employees don't have space for a home office or if they simply need the social or physical infrastructure an office outside the home provides, be willing to cover the costs of a coworking space if your company doesn't have an office location nearby.

Then:

New tools for virtual collaboration are coming out every day. Plus, you need different tools for different purposes—all of which means you'll need to research and try various options to decide what's best for your team. Make sure you've covered the basics like chat, video conferencing, and file sharing (you would be surprised at the number of businesses still trying to use archaic methods for these systems). You also need tools for activities like brainstorming, which require more focus and real-time interaction. Ask your team what they're struggling with and let them have a say in the tools that are selected.

Finally:

Once your team is set up and can successfully collaborate, you can focus on building community. Many businesses have attempted to do this backward. They tried to force people to "engage" while continuously overworking them. If you've hired the right people to be on your team, they are likely to genuinely care about one another. If they aren't overloaded and they feel like their team supports them, they will want to offer support back. This can be emotional support, project support, or both. Encourage interaction, information sharing, and camaraderie.

Take Action

Workers want flexible options, and they're willing to leave if you don't offer an arrangement that works for their lifestyles. Instead of resisting, ask them what they need and *listen*. Once each person has a comfortable work arrangement, focus on collaboration and community.

55. Make Time for Appointments and Commitments

Help People Feel: *Safe*

Harmful Habit: *Unnecessarily Strict Schedules*

Successful Strategy: *Flexibility and Freedom for Personal Care*

What's Gone Wrong

Professional athletes spend most of their time preparing themselves to be in peak condition so that they can perform when they need to. They train, they study, they recover. Business executives love sports metaphors—but in the many analogies thrown around the conference table, no one ever talks about all of the prep and care that goes into actual greatness. That's where work-life balance comes in.

Businesses want greatness all the time. Night and day, day after day, with no time for prep or recovery at all. Demands on employees are so high that they often put off important personal care tasks because they simply don't feel like they can take the time they need. In the worst organizations, employees skip breaks of all kinds, sometimes even bathroom breaks!

How can anyone possibly expect great work from a person who is so over-burdened that they can't even find time to go to the bathroom?!

Basic personal care includes physical health, mental health, essential personal tasks, and sometimes essential personal upkeep. They're all important and they're often only available during daytime work hours. So, don't assume that workers only need to take time for appointments and commitments once in a blue moon. They may even need to take time about once per week.

Here's What to Do

Too many businesses have failed to plan worker capacity appropriately. In #67: Be Honest about Workloads in Chapter 8, there is an explanation of appropriate capacity planning. Good capacity planning should include 20 percent admin time, which should equate to about 7.2 hours per week.

That's a healthy amount of time—enough to take care of employee appointments and commitments. Going forward, operate with the assumption that each employee will need that much time per week to attend various personal events.

Even if you are doing good capacity planning, you can't just assume that people will take the time they need. After all, they've been conditioned not to (see #51: Make Time Off Sacrosanct in Chapter 7). And you're not the only person who might signal to them that it's not okay to do so. Peer pressure is very real. If you have someone on your team who brags about never taking breaks or makes inappropriate comments when others have commitments, you need to address those behaviors with that person. At minimum, they need to know that taking time for commitments is acceptable and encouraged. But the real goal is a culture where no one is watching the door (or your away status). You want an organization of mature, trustworthy adults who support each other.

One additional special note: People who are caregivers to children, seniors, or others who require significant assistance will undoubtedly need more time than other employees. If you fail to accept that reality, it will put the caregivers under extreme strain. It will also cause deep resentment and conflict on your team if others are forced to absorb that strain. Work with them to create realistic work arrangements that allow them to contribute within their real capacity. If they need to transition to part-time work, hire to fill the gap.

Take Action

If you want a healthy, happy team that operates at consistently good performance, they need to be well cared for. This means taking time for necessary tasks, including personal commitments and appointments. Be careful when you do capacity planning so that overflow work isn't being pushed onto anyone. Be open about your perspective and address any unkind peer pressure directly.

56. Offer Appropriate Leave Time

Help People Feel: *Safe*

Harmful Habit: *Demanding People Work When They Need Leave*

Successful Strategy: *Generous, Humane Leave Policies*

What's Gone Wrong

America: First in many things...but definitely not in parental or caregiver support. (We're not big on support in general.)

We are big on work though. Americans pride themselves on their work ethic, sometimes a little too much. Have you ever heard someone proudly (or even regretfully) say, "I was back at work two days after my mother passed away" or "I didn't take any time off for paternity leave"? These sentiments don't benefit us, but they are rooted deep in our collective value system of hard work and independence.

These practices are unhealthy and should not continue. You might think you don't have much influence on that because of state or federal laws governing types of leave. But those laws define the *minimum* standards. It's your company's choice if it's going to simply follow them (a.k.a., do the bare minimum) or if it's going to set policies that are more compassionate and employee friendly.

Here's What to Do

There are many forms of leave. Some are short-term and others are longer. Some are legally regulated and some are cultural norms. Here are four forms of leave that are particularly difficult for workers. Make sure you know your company's basic policy on each one, then promote as kind and generous a definition or interpretation as you possibly can when they arise.

Parental Leave

Defining a generous parental leave policy benefits your workers, your business, and society at large. *All* parents should be encouraged to take significant time off. (We still have a massive amount of work to do as a society to reach gender equity in parenting, and leaves for all parents will help that.) Yes, you *have* to follow FMLA requirements. But you *can* do more than that. Set a generous amount of time, pay as much as you can, and make sure it's offered to all parents. The costs are a drop in the proverbial bucket.

Bereavement Leave

The state of bereavement leave is, frankly, shocking. Often, workers are given only three days for an immediate family member and one day for a non-immediate family member. How can anyone honestly say that three days is enough time to grieve a parent, spouse, or child? If you are in a position to set or influence these policies, think about what a justifiable amount of time would be. Supporting an employee in such a difficult time is certainly the right thing to do.

Caregiver Leave

Like parental leave, caregivers are not being given sufficient support. Depending on the situation and who they are caring for, caregivers may need more ongoing flexibility. Work openly with the person, try hard to understand their situation, and then have policies in place that are supportive. Talk frequently with your employee to gauge their short- and long-term needs. Fair treatment is nonnegotiable. Don't make life harder for someone who is doing their best to care for a person who needs it.

Personal Leaves of Absence

It's impossible to imagine every scenario that could possibly come up for your team. For other situations that arise, do you have good policies in place? It's better to allow someone time when they need it than it is to lose them. Most policies are so tight and unforgiving. Yours doesn't have to be.

Take Action

Current leave policies are often built to offer the bare minimum. They're business-centric, not employee-centric. Lead your company's quest for change and be as compassionate and flexible as you can.

57. Stop Rewarding Face Time

Help People Feel: *Valued*

Harmful Habit: *Pressure to Be In Person All the Time*

Successful Strategy: *Real Relationships Based on Trust*

What's Gone Wrong

The world of finance in particular has long been the pinnacle of "face time"—the idea that showing your face holds a superior importance, often even more than hard skills (and *certainly* more than soft skills). After all, at some point, your boss is going to come out on "the floor" and expect to see you at your desk. There are the lunch meetings, the golf outings, the evening galas. If you're there, you get a point on their mental scoreboard. If you're not, you might as well not exist. After 7 p.m., the point system goes up to time-and-a-half. (Everyone knows that's when you earn the real points.)

While face time is intended to encourage hard work and dedication, it has many other consequences. It is, by nature, exclusionary. Being in the office for long hours is only possible for people that have the resources to do so. If you're a primary caregiver to children or you are reliant on public transportation, it may be simply impossible. That means that face time is disproportionally difficult for women, who average significantly more parenting duties. We know that we want a more diverse workforce, but pushing face time doesn't support that. It makes it more difficult for outsiders to make their way "in."

Here's What to Do

The truth is that relying on face time is extremely lazy. You're hoping that institutional knowledge will simply "rub off" as a result of prolonged proximity. What's that they say? Hope is not a strategy...?

Dispersed, diverse teams are going to win in the next era of business. So it's time to be *intentional* about training, mentoring, and communication.

Instead of:	Do this:
Forcing people into an office so that they can "absorb information."	Make more systemic, formal plans for sharing knowledge.
Assessing dedication based on number of hours and willingness to "show up."	Form a real relationship, listen to your team members, and understand their motivations and goals.
Hoping that new employees will learn from senior employees "on the job."	Create a formal mentorship program with real mentor training and standards.

Take Action

Face time is a business norm that was used for decades to assess dedication and pass down institutional knowledge. However, it is no longer realistic and is more of a liability than an asset. Instead of continuing to try to force face time to happen, invest your time in intentional training, mentorship, and communication.

58. Stop Letting Your Employees Absorb All of the Problems

Help People Feel: *Respected*

Harmful Habit: *Forcing Employees to Offset Systemic Organizational Problems*

Successful Strategy: *Fair, Balanced Expectations and Workloads*

What's Gone Wrong

Leaders can be slow to recognize and react to the overflowing workloads of the people under them. When you're a dozen levels removed from the people who actually do all of the work, it's easy to ignore what's really going on. If everyone is just a number on a spreadsheet, then you lose your sense of perspective. This is why some executives are sluggish—or even obstinate—about properly investing in salaries, tools, and other resources. It doesn't affect *them*. To them, forcing three people to do the work of five is a huge success. Think of the savings!

But down on the ground level, most good-natured people are filling in the cracks. They're rushing and hustling to get it all done. Because, if they don't, they'll get in trouble. They'll also feel disappointed in themselves, even though they were set up to fail.

That's what's happening on a massive scale. People are being taken advantage of and it's compromising their mental and physical health. The issue is that these problems are systemic to the organization—and they need to be fixed at that level too.

No matter where your leadership role falls within your organization, you can provide some protection from the constant crunch that comes down from above. You can do that in three ways.

Stop Blaming Organizational Problems on Employees

You've probably been conditioned to look for blame on your team. You're being asked to rate their performance and admonish them if they fail, even if that failure isn't their fault. Unlearning this behavior takes some effort. Instead of just looking at employee performance, look at the broader context. Are the expectations realistic? Do they have the tools to succeed? If you don't fix the problems at the source, there's only so much each employee can do. Don't blame them—spend your time addressing the bigger problems instead.

Communicate Upward and Advocate Loudly

Hierarchical separation is one of the main villains in this story. One of the reasons that distant executives don't do anything about major problems is they don't know about them. You can fix that. Be loud in communicating up the chain. Advocate for budget and resources. Bring hard numbers to explain your points and don't back down.

Don't Add to the Pressure

It can be tempting to condemn this behavior in others but to view your own additions as harmless. It's just one more little thing, isn't it? Maybe. Before you dump a new project or process on your team, estimate how much work it is going to be and where it fits into the overall priority list. If you have to add something but there's no open capacity, then take something off of the list first.

Take Action

Employees have absorbed so many organizational problems and filled so many careless cracks that they're unable to carry anymore. Use your leadership and communication skills to make sure the higher-ups know about these systemic problems so they can be addressed on that level.

59. Honor Needs for Privacy

Help People Feel: *Safe*

Harmful Habit: *Invasive Questions*

Successful Strategy: *Respect for Boundaries*

What's Gone Wrong

Should your work life and personal life ever mix? Or should there be an iron wall that separates them? Perspectives on work-life crossover are changing—again. And not in the way you might think.

For many, the prevailing advice for a long time was to keep work and life separate. Employees' work lives had to be pristinely *professional* (meaning, devoid of all personality). So they adopted work personas. Their work personas used the dreaded "telephone voice" when they spoke. They dressed in bland ties and soul-sucking pantyhose that shrouded any little bits of personal lives that people might accidentally bring to work. And they absolutely *did not* share anything about their personal lives.

Then the after-work softball leagues came along. The break room was filled with pizza (allegedly a "party"). And suddenly Cheryl from HR wanted to open every meeting with a personal check-in, a.k.a. a work-appropriate review of your weekend activities. In the 2000s and early 2010s, this initially seemed quite refreshing. A boss who was actually interested in you as a whole person? How novel.

But gradually, these personal crossovers started to feel less liberating and more invasive. If I want to spend my whole weekend bingeing shows and scrolling my phone, what business is that of yours, Cheryl?

As people reevaluate their relationships with work, privacy needs and personal boundaries evolve. And they are becoming more—you guessed it—personal.

Here's What to Do

You probably have your own preferences with what you like to share at work and what you don't. You probably also have a long history of various mentors/bosses/family members telling you what you should and shouldn't do. There are very real, long-ranging mores that are hard to let go of.

Despite the changes that we've seen over many years, what we haven't seen is much respect for individual preferences. Typically it is the boss (or some other authority figure) setting the standards for the whole team. The boss bases the standards on their personal preferences and what feels right to them. Assumptions are made and they aren't always correct.

The bottom line is that people should get to decide how much they want to share at work. As the boss, you need to be sensitive to the signals your team members are sending. Even if you think you're "just being friendly," you might make someone uncomfortable. So don't push it if they are slow to share. If you have team members who are the opposite, you should respect that too. If they want to share their hiking photos or tell you about a family event, be interested and friendly.

Take Action

Not everyone has the same work-life boundaries. Some people want to share, and others don't. Either way, as the leader, you should respect their preferences. You never truly know what someone has going on at home, so take the cues you're given.

60. Be Parent Friendly

Help People Feel: *Safe*

Harmful Habit: *False Preconceptions That Limit Opportunities*

Successful Strategy: *Fair Choices*

What's Gone Wrong

Parenting is hard work—especially today with all of the expectations, enlightenment, and judgment. The majority of families with children have two working parents. As they say, you're expected to work like you don't have children and parent like you don't have a job. Sounds simple, right?

Building a parent-friendly workplace is good for society. It helps all parents be active, present, and able to contribute equitably at home. It helps children get their needs met while also allowing for healthy parental relationships. Those things, in turn, move us toward a safer, healthier society.

To be clear, being parent friendly doesn't mean that parents should get special treatment while others pick up the slack. It means having appropriate resources and opportunities that allow parents to contribute fully. There has been a lot of tension between the childless and the parent communities because managers essentially pit them against one another. That comes back to poor planning and staffing, leading to situations where there isn't enough coverage.

Parent-friendly policies can benefit everyone. There's no reason that flexible work arrangements, healthy expectations, and ample support can't be offered to everyone.

Here's What to Do

Here's a golden tip to live by: Let parents (and all people, really) make their own decisions. Don't decide for them. Here's what that means: Let's say that you have a person on your team who's a brand-new parent. They're going through the trials and tribulations that come with tiny humans, which can be quite exhausting. This person is talented and there's a promotion opportunity that they're eligible for. Should you consider them? Or would it be nicer to let them focus on parenting and give the extra responsibility to someone else?

There's no way for you to know—you need to ask the person. When you make assumptions, you could either put too much on their plate or cut them off from an opportunity that might be critical for their future. Each person is different. Some may not be ready to take on new responsibility when they have young kids or to take an overseas assignment when they have teenagers—while others might welcome the chance. (Truthfully, this applies to nonparents too: They might not fit into stereotypes just because they're childless.)

Changing the opportunities you offer to someone based on their parental status is discrimination. It's also a systemic way to dampen women's upward mobility, since they're more burdened by parenting responsibilities. Instead of cutting off opportunities people didn't even know they had, be open and nonjudgmental. Ask them if they want to take the project or role, and make sure they know that you support their decision no matter what it may be.

Take Action

We aren't doing a good job supporting parents in the workplace, which is a systemic burden for parents, especially women. Staff appropriately so that you have adequate person power and can offer flexibility. Most importantly, even if you think someone would have certain preferences because of their parental status, offer them the opportunities they deserve and let them decide for themselves. No guilt trips allowed.

chapter 8

Support Mental Health

The priorities of mental health and those of the workplace are often in direct conflict. Your mental health wants you to take a break, but the workplace wants you to keep going. Mental health strives for balance and peace, but the workplace strives for drive and endurance. Does success in one area have to mean failure in the other?

If you look at the past, the answer is yes. The picture of a model worker has been someone who never takes breaks, never has needs, never asks for help, and never gives up. Coincidentally, that is also the recipe for a stress-induced heart attack. So, instead, let's look at the future.

In the future, the most successful businesses will be fueled with creativity and heart. They will be staffed by people who care about their customers and also about the world in general. Good mental health won't be a detriment; it will be a necessity. Because there is no way that people can feel good in the workplace if they don't have a healthy mental and emotional baseline.

This chapter will focus on ways you can support your team's mental health by both finding the right opportunities to allow different individuals to flourish and by challenging or removing things that are detrimental to mental health in the workplace.

61. Ditch Mental Health Stigma

Help People Feel: *Safe*

Harmful Habit: *Outdated Ideas That Prevent People from Getting Help*

Successful Strategy: *Healthy, Open Support*

What's Gone Wrong

Human understanding of mental health has always been changing. Views on this topic have changed so dramatically from even twenty years ago. As with many other areas of healthcare, we can expect to see much, much more advancement in the years to come.

Likewise, personal understanding of mental health is always changing and expanding as well. Everyone was taught, either directly or indirectly, a certain way to understand mental health. Some people were taught the basics of mental health; others learned it's taboo or you're "weak" if you discuss it.

Unfortunately, these vestiges of mental health stigma are still lingering. You might have one of these archetypes haunting your office:

The Scoffer	The Blamer	The Punisher
Rolls their eyes and mocks any mention of mental health needs	Blames mental health issues on someone's habits or mindset	Threatens consequences for admitting to mental health needs
Refuses to acknowledge that mental health conditions are real	Thinks a person can "get over it" and that they should "deal with it"	Has an "all or nothing" mindset
Views mental health support as a sign of weakness	Says "we've all been there" and refuses to acknowledge that people need real treatment or support	May come from the military, medical fields, or other backgrounds where mental health needs are punished

It's one thing to have privately held beliefs—each person has a right to choose how they wish to care for themselves. However, if someone in your organization is acting aggressively and insultingly toward others, that is a form of bullying. These behaviors need to be shut down immediately.

Here's What to Do

Just as with physical health, mental health is foundational to a safe, happy workplace. Your job as a leader is to carefully consider mental health needs and show your team members that you take supporting their mental health seriously.

There may also be times when you may need to actively encourage mental healthcare. If you notice that someone is struggling with symptoms that could indicate depression, anxiety, or other challenges, offer support. While you should never make them disclose their health conditions, you can ask if they need help. Respect their privacy while also being supportive.

Make it clear to all your team members that you recognize mental health as an essential priority. If someone asks for help, take them seriously and follow through. Social acceptance of mental healthcare helps increase access to and utilization of mental health services. You can be part of the solution by making sure mental health isn't taboo at your workplace and advocating for good mental health coverage in your benefits package.

Take Action

Though things are improving, there is still a lot of bias, shame, and stigma associated with mental health. Taking care of your mental health is just as important as taking care of your physical health. As a leader, you play a role in supporting the mental health of your team. Don't let anyone become a bully on topics related to mental health, and openly show your acceptance of mental healthcare. If someone needs support, make it a top priority.

62. Consider Going to Therapy (and Encourage Others to Do the Same)

Help People Feel: *Safe*

Harmful Habit: *Lack of Support for Mental Healthcare*

Successful Strategy: *Open, Honest Access to Therapy*

What's Gone Wrong

Therapy is an important component of mental healthcare. There are many types of therapists out there, and they specialize in every imaginable area. Thankfully, more and more people are seeking their help each year. Even so, many more people might hold back for one reason or another—like the stigma of seeing a therapist or the demands of work.

Therapy should be accessible and well utilized. While it is important for people to care for themselves, they also deserve to benefit from the support of a professional. It will help them reflect on who they are and who they want to be. That's extremely important for both personal and professional development.

Here's What to Do

People with all sorts of mental health conditions can be wonderfully successful in the workplace, especially with the right care. The hiccup is that often that care needs to happen during the workday. Most therapists are only available during daytime hours or offer only a limited number of morning, evening, or weekend hours. That math just doesn't add up, especially if we want more people to be able to access therapy.

So, if at all possible, allow people on your team to take time to seek mental health support. That may mean that they're unavailable for 1–2 daytime hours each week. What does that really cost you? Assuming they're flexing their time, it costs virtually nothing. A worker who has a stronger mental health foundation is happier, more creative, and better able to manage stress—exactly the type of person you want on your team.

As the team leader, you too are facing a lot of pressure and almost certainly have a busy life. Many people are counting on you for support. *You* might want to consider talking to someone about your responsibilities and the demands of your job. Making time for therapy is like putting on your oxygen mask before assisting others: You're getting what you need so that you can be there when others need you.

Going to therapy for the first time can sound intimidating. For some, it may even seem frighteningly like admitting weakness. But that's like saying that going to the gym means you're out of shape. If you've been scared away from doing something that will ultimately make you healthier, it only limits your support system and access to care. One of the best reasons to go to therapy is to destigmatize it for yourself and others around you. You'll experience the process, which will make it less intimidating. If you're comfortable with doing so, being public about attending therapy is hugely beneficial for everyone. It requires you to be vulnerable and open to judgment, but it also allows you to be a significant role model and active part of normalizing mental healthcare.

Take Action

Trying out therapy can make you a better leader and role model. It can be difficult to schedule therapy around a corporate schedule, so embrace flexibility when you can. Make sure that your team members also have the opportunity to get mental health support. Treat them with respect and trust them to take care of themselves while still performing their job well.

63. Protect Your Introverts

Help People Feel: *Safe*

Harmful Habit: *Loud, Invasive Discomfort*

Successful Strategy: *Quiet, Calm, and Focus*

What's Gone Wrong

The work-from-home revolution has been an enormous boon for introverts. Do your chosen job from a comfortable home environment without the distractions of the office? It's a homebody's dream come true!

Introversion-extroversion is a wide spectrum. Some people identify as true introverts or extroverts. But most are somewhere in the middle, though they likely have introvert or extrovert tendencies. Some even identify as ambiverts, meaning that they may feel more introverted or extroverted depending on their mood and context.

Culturally, we're increasingly shifting toward introversion. Technology has brought so many conveniences, like shipping and delivery—but those little luxuries come with opportunities to self-isolate. Is it any wonder that people feel more anxious about social situations if they almost never have to even go into a store? In fact, research shows that our social brain behaves like a muscle. The more we exercise it, the stronger it becomes. The opposite is also true: The more we remove ourselves from social situations, the more challenging and overwhelming they can seem.

Before you assume that this trend toward introversion is a completely bad thing, think about this: Life has become exponentially more complicated in other ways. With all of the struggle and mounting expectations, can you honestly blame someone for needing more time to themselves?

Here's What to Do

It isn't your place as a leader to judge your team members' introverted/extroverted nature. Your job is to build a healthy, safe environment for everyone.

Remember, introverts have many gifts to offer! But encouraging them to open up isn't just a matter of asking. You're going to need to earn their trust, which takes time and consistency. Introverts often feel like they don't fit into environments where loud voices seem to be the most rewarded and social prowess is valued just as much as (and sometimes more than) competence. As Susan Cain, author of *Quiet: The Power of Introverts in a World That Can't Stop Talking*, notes, "There's zero correlation between being the best talker and having the best ideas." Here are some simple tips for protecting your introverts:

○ **Offer private ways for them to share their thoughts and ideas.** For example, instead of only listening to what is said spontaneously in a meeting, give equal weight to ideas submitted separately in writing.

○ **Don't always expect an immediate response.** Introverts need more time to process their ideas and emotions, and they prefer to do so independently.

○ **Pause frequently and check in.** Don't assume that everyone will jump right into the conversation without prompting. And *especially* don't assume that all of the best ideas are being said out loud.

○ **Share structure and expectations in advance.** Introverts like to have time to prepare so that they aren't caught off guard.

○ **Watch out for "introvert bullying."** Don't let peers or other leaders put your introverts down. Show them that their style and perspective are truly valued.

Take Action

Whether you consider yourself to be an introvert, extrovert, or something in between, you must have respect for the social needs of others. It costs you and the company nothing to offer introverts more time and space to be themselves. With the right environment (and thoughtful leadership), introverts will feel much more comfortable being themselves and contributing fully to their teams.

64. Fuel Your Extroverts

Help People Feel: *Safe*
Harmful Habit: *Stiff, Oppressive Environment*
Successful Strategy: *Space for Extroverts to Thrive*

What's Gone Wrong

Lights down. Music up. Time to get *loud* and talk about fueling your extroverts. You know your extroverts—they're positively unmissable. In fact, if you listen hard, you can probably hear them organizing a happy hour right now.

Like true introverts, true extroverts are rare. However, unlike introverts, who prefer to hang back, extroverts need others to be fulfilled. They need social stimulation and interaction to feel their best. It's your job as the leader to ensure those needs are met in a healthy and productive way.

While introverts have found more advantages in the last few years (see the previous entry), many extroverts have found themselves climbing the walls. They struggled through months, even years, of reduced social opportunities. Many extroverts *hated* working from home. And when the work from home era finally ended, they returned to offices that were full of nothing but dusty chairs and moldy old coffee.

Even though extroverts are outgoing, don't assume they can or will take care of their own needs without your help. There simply may not be enough opportunities to do so. And even if they seem magnanimous and effervescent, that doesn't mean that they don't sometimes feel lonely or sad. Extroverts need just as much care as everyone else.

Extroverts can be creative powerhouses. Their vigor and joy can be infectious, especially when they feel supported and valued. To unlock their full potential, you need to give extroverts the freedom to be themselves. Show them that you understand their need to interact and respect their ability to bring people together.

Here are some simple tips for fueling your extroverts:

- **Be willing to talk.** Get to know them, including their interests, hobbies, and families. Don't act like this conversation is a burden to you or a waste of your time. They need strong social bonds to thrive, so be genuine.

- **If possible, find opportunities to meet in person.** Whether it's meeting regularly for lunch or seeing each other at an annual event, time together will be appreciated.

- **Invest in your relationship.** Extroverts don't like feeling like work is purely transactional. They want to see and be seen.

- **Gently balance any dominating behavior with kind reminders that others need opportunities to contribute.** Extroverts usually don't mean to ignore others, but they can sometimes forget that not everyone is comfortable speaking openly.

- **Applaud their creative energy.** Let them know that their personality and energy are a welcome addition to the team.

Take Action

While extroverts have had a long history of performing well in the workplace, recent changes have left them starved for the social fuel they need. Now is the time to take special care of your extroverts, especially if you work in a virtual or hybrid business where social opportunities are limited. When extroverts feel socially charged, they are unstoppable buoys that pull everyone up. Your job as a leader is to create the environment they need to feel comfortable and appreciated.

65. Acknowledge Microaggressions

Help People Feel: *Safe*

Harmful Habit: *Small Reminders of Entrenched Power Structures*

Successful Strategy: *Allowing Everyone to Belong*

What's Gone Wrong

The term "microaggression" was coined by Dr. Chester M. Pierce and describes small, frequent actions and language that emphasize the disparity between a group with power and a marginalized group. While it is no longer socially acceptable to be overtly discriminatory, microaggressions often go completely unchecked. Microaggressions are 100 percent real and are constant, destabilizing attacks on marginalized groups. They also reinforce a message you don't want to send: that certain people don't belong.

What do microaggressions look and sound like? This chart adapted from the National Education Association shows you some common examples.

EXAMPLES OF MICROAGGRESSIONS

Theme	Microaggression	Message
Ascription of intelligence	"You are so articulate."	It's unusual for someone of your race to be intelligent.
Denial of individual racism	"My best friend is Black."	I'm not racist because I have friends of color. (This is sometimes called the "proximity defense.")

Disrespect	More prestigious projects are assigned to male workers than female workers.	The contributions of female workers are less worthy than the contributions of male workers.
Myth of meritocracy	"Men and women have equal opportunities for achievement."	The playing field is even, so if women cannot make it, the problem is with them.
Endorsement of heteronormative culture and behaviors	"Do you have a wife/husband?"	I am expecting you to be heterosexual or straight because that is normal.
Denial of bodily privacy	To a transgender person: "What surgeries have you had?"	You are different or abnormal, so I am going to objectify your body and ask you inappropriate questions.

Adapted from: National Education Association,
www.nea.org/sites/default/files/2021-02/Examples%20of%20Microaggressions.pdf.

Here's What to Do

If you hear any of these examples, you must take immediate action. Make it clear that these comments and beliefs are not permitted in your workplace by correcting misconceptions and directly addressing insulting statements. These are not "opinions" and there are not "two sides" here. They are acts of discrimination and are harmful, both to people's career and to their mental health.

Take Action

Microaggressions are very real and very harmful. For a long time, we've excused them as "not a big deal" or told people that they should be "less sensitive." If you're going to build a workplace that is safe for everyone, you must acknowledge and shut down microaggressions. At the systemic level, ensure that your company has a robust diversity, equity, inclusion, and belonging program that offers educational opportunities and creates environments for people to come together to talk about various marginalized groups' experiences and needs.

66. Stop Relying On the EAP

Help People Feel: *Valued*

Harmful Habit: *Outsourced Support*

Successful Strategy: *Personal Support*

What's Gone Wrong

Good old employee assistance programs (EAPs). They're supposed to be helpful, but are they? EAPs typically come from an external provider, like Justworks or ADP. Here are a few forms of "assistance" EAPs commonly offer:

○ Counseling for serious issues like addiction or trauma

○ Assistance finding childcare, eldercare, and other forms of family care

○ Basic legal and financial advice

○ Adoption support

○ Assistance finding a mental health professional (and sometimes they offer a limited number of free counseling sessions)

On paper, this is all good! The problem is that actual EAP usage is extremely low. But businesses point to it like a "get out of jail free" card when anyone complains about benefits. You're most likely to hear about the EAP if you or someone on your team is struggling. Instead of directly offering support, HR pipes up and says, "Our EAP can help with that," and they give you a phone number to call. Are you going to call it? Only about 10 percent of employees do.

Despite knowing that employees are unlikely to seek and find help this way, the business usually steps back at this point and considers the matter resolved. But read that list again. These are serious, often chronic, complex issues that are not going to be resolved in one phone call. Should you stop offering an EAP? No. But you *should* stop relying on it as the only source of support.

Here's What to Do

When businesses dismiss employee struggles by simply referring them to an outside company, they aren't treating them in a very humane way. It's rather procedural if you think about it: Employee expresses distress → refer them to the EAP → move on to the next "problem."

When you treat people this way, they don't feel valued. It can even feel dehumanizing. You're writing off their life's greatest challenges without actually *doing* anything about it yourself.

Ask Them What They Need from You

No one struggling with addiction or fertility trauma can just go about their business like everyone else. If you know that they're going through something serious, small accommodations (and sometimes larger ones) can make a big difference. Do they need to change their schedule? Do they want you to ask others to respect their privacy and not ask them about their situation? Ask them what they need and do your best to make it happen.

Be Part of Their Support Network

It's rare that someone considers their boss to be part of their support network. That's because most bosses are removed from an employee's personal life. You don't want to overstep, but you do want to show that you actually care. It takes time, but prove that you are someone that they can trust. Did they need to take time off? Let them do so without invasive questions. Are they struggling to keep their head above water? Recognize that "above and beyond" isn't realistic for them right now. You can't do everything, but do what you can.

Take Action

Employee assistance programs are a nice benefit to offer employees. But leaders and HR professionals can't use them as an excuse to not personally offer support to employees who need it. Asking for help (or even admitting that you need it) is exceptionally hard, particularly in the workplace. If someone needs help, give it.

67. Be Honest about Workloads

Help People Feel: *Respected*

Harmful Habit: *Systemically Overworked Employees Who Can't Take a Break*

Successful Strategy: *Realistic Workloads*

What's Gone Wrong

Businesses and bosses are routinely dishonest about workloads. They say things like "family first" and "employee-centric" but, mostly, it's all talk. They pile on unrealistically, knowing that most employees will just find a way to get it all done, even at the cost of their own mental health.

Why does this happen? Part of it comes back to the "squeezing" we've talked about several times so far. But it isn't just aggression, it's also bad math.

Even hardworking "above and beyond" employees only have so many good hours in a day. A person might be able to stretch out their productivity for bursts of time. But that is not sustainable. Nor is it responsible labor planning.

Healthy, realistic labor planning and workload distribution accounts for:

- Paid time off
- Meeting time
- Admin time
- Learning time

Unless you're in a scrum work environment (meaning, one where every task is awarded a number of points and formally prioritized before it is assigned to workers, as with engineers), it's unlikely that your workload planning accounts for all of these.

Here's What to Do

If you want healthy, responsibly planned workloads, then you need to do some math and figure out how much work is getting done every week. Let's use a typical individual contributor as an example.

TOTAL WORK HOURS PER WEEK: 40

Individual Contributor Time	50%	20 Hours
Meeting Time	20%	8 Hours
Admin Time	20%	8 Hours
Learning Time	10%	4 Hours

So that means that for every individual contributor on your team, there are twenty hours per week of person power, right? Wrong. You're making a very common error. You're assuming that a typical week doesn't contain any PTO or breaks.

There are two ways you could responsibly account for time off: macroplanning or microplanning. First, let's look at macroplanning. When you're planning for the "big picture," you can estimate approximate PTO use throughout the year. To do that, let's assume fifteen days of PTO, plus ten vacation days (which should be the bare minimum). That's five weeks out of the year, or about 10 percent. This allows us to recalculate.

TOTAL WORK HOURS PER WEEK: 36
(PTO SPREAD EVENLY ACROSS THE YEAR)

Individual Contributor Time	50%	18 Hours
Meeting Time	20%	7.2 Hours
Admin Time	20%	7.2 Hours
Learning Time	10%	3.6 Hours

This math is significantly more accurate. It works if you're trying to decide how many people you need on the team (or, the opposite: how many person-hours of work the team can perform).

But people don't usually take their PTO in such small increments. This is why you also need to do some microplanning. To keep things simple, instead of assuming that your people are each using 10 percent of their PTO, we'll assume that 10 percent of your people are on PTO at any given time. This means, if you employ ten people on your team, you effectively have nine people working at any given time.

Many businesses want to ignore these numbers, which is why their employees feel like they can *never* take time off. They're absorbing the extra 10 percent—along with the extra stress and lack of sleep. That's not a recipe for good mental health.

Take Action

Don't delude yourself into thinking that every person on your team will be able to work forty full hours per week. It's probably more like eighteen after you account for PTO, meeting time, admin time, and learning time. Keep this in mind when planning how much you expect your team to accomplish. Having realistic expectations is one way to show your employees that their stress levels and mental health matter to you.

68. Shut Down Fake Emergencies

Help People Feel: *Respected*

Harmful Habit: *A Constant State of Emergency*

Successful Strategy: *A Safe, Calm Environment*

What's Gone Wrong

What do offices and reality shows have in common? Drama is always going down. And much like in a reality show, virtually all of these "high stakes" office situations are completely fake.

Somewhere along the way, companies started treating *everything* like an emergency, whether it truly is one or not. The workplace has become dominated by panic. Managers squeeze and rush their employees into exhaustion, demanding "above and beyond" performance for average (or worse) salaries.

The biggest problem is that this has become the default state. They think that, by creating a sense of urgency, they're getting more out of each employee. Worse, they treat people like an endlessly renewable resource that can give and give with no limit.

There's always *someone* who will react when the "emergency" occurs. But instead of encouraging employees to keep things in perspective, they (either consciously or subconsciously) encourage the hysteria. Instead of releasing the pressure, they pour more on. Sometimes this is done with negative reinforcement ("If you don't get this done, we'll lose this client!"). Other times, through positive reinforcement ("The executive team is going to be so impressed when they see how resilient you are."). Either way, this style of workflow is disingenuously pushing people past their limits.

Here's What to Do

Think of the last time you faced a *real* emergency at work. It's probably only happened a handful of times. However, you've probably been *told* that there was an emergency more times than you can count—multiple times per week at some points.

Once this happens, the word "emergency" (along with "important" and "urgent") loses all meaning. So, in order to separate the real emergencies from the fake emergencies, you need to redefine what an emergency is.

There are two things that define a real emergency: consequences and timing.

O **Consequences:** There must be real, specific, known, and severe consequences.

O **Timing:** There must be concrete, clear timing that is driving the situation.

With this in mind, let's differentiate some real emergencies from fake emergencies. But before we do, bear in mind that true emergencies in the corporate world are extremely rare. In other industries, like healthcare and social services, they are much more frequent.

Real Emergency	Fake Emergency
Someone is in severe danger or distress.	Someone is very angry.
Critical services or materials are unavailable.	Something is overdue.
Serious disruption or risk to security or infrastructure.	Disruption in processes or workflows.
Sudden, unexpected change in conditions that may cause imminent harm.	Failure to plan ahead.

When you look at this chart, it seems extremely obvious, doesn't it? The fake emergencies are driven by ego or are hiccups that can be resolved. Real emergencies are rooted in safety. If you sense a fake emergency that is causing panic, address it calmly. It may help to say, "It's concerning that this has happened, but before we divert resources, let's determine what needs to be done and where this fits into current priorities."

Take Action

Many businesses or even industries (ahem, marketing) operate in a constant state of "emergency." However, these situations often result in inconvenience, not true imminent or current danger. In business, true emergencies are extremely rare and can be identified by both severe consequences and concrete timing. Everything else is just impatience in disguise.

69. Understand Individual Communication Needs

Help People Feel: *Respected*

Harmful Habit: *Haphazard, Selfish Communication*

Successful Strategy: *Thoughtful, Personalized Communication*

What's Gone Wrong

Businesses move fast these days, so the stream of communication is rapid and constant. It's overwhelming for everyone and we're all just trying to keep our heads above water. As a result, we sometimes fail to communicate thoughtfully, which at best is confusing and at worst can feel disrespectful or even threatening to others.

Keep in mind that our collective sensitivity to unpleasant communication is higher than it used to be. Punctuation is practically a symbol of the generational divide. And that isn't even considering emojis. We're all so swamped and rushed that we reply superfast (and almost never reread things before we send them)... but we're also extremely quick to perceive aggression or insincerity (which could easily arise from a hastily written message). It's a tough combination.

The good news is that this doesn't have to be a mysterious puzzle to decode. You can ask people what their preferences are and adjust your communications accordingly.

The tricky thing is sometimes overriding your own preferences in favor of the needs of others. Maybe you're an email person and hate picking up the phone. Well, if your key employee is a phone person, you're going to need to be more flexible.

Here's What to Do

Take time to ask the people on your team about their communication preferences. Ask about the following topics:

- **Time of day:** When do they prefer to communicate? What times of day are best for meetings or discussions? What times are off-limits? Some people are early risers and others prefer to meet later in the day. It doesn't cost you anything to respect those needs.

- **Channels:** There are so many communication channels these days and everyone has their preferences. What does your team member prefer? Even better, why do they prefer that?

- **Response time:** Some people are quick responders and others need time to process. If you know that someone is a processor, don't demand an immediate response from them on nonurgent matters. It's unrealistic and unnecessary.

- **Style:** We all communicate differently. Some people need information quickly and directly. Others feel used if you don't take time to connect before diving in. You certainly have a style and so does everyone else. It's best to simply ask and then take those requests seriously.

Once you've established healthy, beneficial communication with the individuals on your team, it's time to think about the larger group. Are there some core principles that would benefit everyone? For example, what is the generally accepted turnaround time for responding to an email? Can everyone try to reread their messages once before sending them? Are there core hours of communication that they should stay within? It will take some work, but it is possible to set 4–5 basic guidelines about respectful and beneficial communication.

Take Action

Everyone says communication is important, but very few do it well. One easy way to improve communication within your team is to ask the people on your team about their preferences. Once you're communicating effectively in one-on-one situations, work on the group's communication standards. Agreeing on clear, respectful guidelines will work wonders.

70. Give Better Feedback

Help People Feel: *Respected*

Harmful Habit: *Biased, Superficial Feedback*

Successful Strategy: *Genuinely Helpful Support*

What's Gone Wrong

Feedback is important. The problem is that the feedback methods most commonly used today are extremely biased, poorly delivered, and unhelpful. Poorly delivered feedback won't help an employee improve. But it will viciously attack their mental health, stealing their confidence and amping up their anxiety.

A typical performance review is conducted by a person's manager. There might be a self-review component, but anything else—peer reviews, for example—is very rare. We already know that leadership levels do not have adequate diversity. Additionally, these managers are rarely trained on developing others and almost never trained on the qualities to look for in potential promotees. So, instead of giving high-quality feedback and promoting diverse candidates with real leadership skills, these managers are doing their best...which usually just amounts to giving feedback on likability and conformity.

Likability is one of the biggest problems in the way feedback is currently given. The qualities that make someone "likable" don't necessarily have anything to do with job performance. They are extremely superficial, and they successfully distract the feedback giver from what actually matters. This is why you have tips floating around about "dressing for the job you want" or "executive presence," both of which are poor predictors of success. Instead of critiquing the way someone dresses, speaks, and sucks up, people should be encouraged to grow hard and soft skills that actually matter.

Work on giving better feedback that will help people grow in more meaningful and equitable ways. Here are three ways to do that.

Use More Objective Measures

If possible, use hard data as a significant source of feedback. This does not mean turning to 360 surveys, where several people ranked above, alongside, and below an employee rate them in various categories. Those can be just as biased as manager feedback. Hard data could be something like sales numbers, number of completed tickets, or some form of measurable growth. These are the actual results of someone's work, which should be their real performance measure.

Eliminate Coded Statements

Part of biased feedback is coded statements. When you hear that someone is being called "abrasive" or "too loud," you should be on red alert because those things are code for "different." Coded statements are especially detrimental to women and People of Color because there are double standards for the genders and races. If you hear these or find yourself using them, investigate carefully and thoroughly. What are you really saying? Is that point actually affecting the person's job performance?

Be Honest and Candid

In what could be an effort to be kind and gentle, sometimes negative feedback gets watered down to the point of being useless. (Everyone knows that the compliment in the feedback sandwich is there to soften the blow.) Instead of dressing it up or saying anything you don't truly mean, be genuine in your feedback. This method may seem uncomfortable at first but is actually the clearest and best way to deliver difficult information.

Take Action

Try to use objective data to measure performance, and deliver it as clearly as possible. Be aware of and on the lookout for potential biases and coded statements so you can remove them from your feedback. Your goal as a leader is to help people get better at their strengths, be aware of their weaknesses, and grow in ways that benefit them and the company.

chapter 9

Foster an Open, Collaborative Group

Your team is your ultimate responsibility as a leader. Whether it is large or small, the health of your team will determine the success of your business.

The challenge is that teams are complicated. Every person on the team has different goals, preferences, and experiences. They need each other, but that doesn't mean they understand one another. There's a reason that interpersonal group dynamics are such an important part of business programs: Enabling a high-functioning team is one of the best things you can do to make your business a success. Remember, nothing big happens without a team.

In this chapter, you will learn the skills and conditions needed to facilitate good teamwork and real collaboration. It's challenging work that even the most seasoned leaders must approach carefully and frequently. When you get it right, the payoff is enormous. Not only will the individual team members feel more supported and satisfied with their work environment, but they'll also have opportunities to inspire one another. Those unique experiences can actually be extremely complementary (if they're shared earnestly and thoughtfully). When real openness and collaboration happen, team members can learn from each other, care for each other, and create amazing things together.

This chapter is all about developing positive relationships within your team to create a workplace culture that feels open, collaborative, inclusive, and encourages people to do their best and support one another to be successful.

71. Value Relationships

Help People Feel: *Valued*

Harmful Habit: *Taking People for Granted*

Successful Strategy: *Strong, Well-Maintained Relationships*

What's Gone Wrong

At the end of the day, what matters most to you? Is it productivity, efficiency, and profit...or is it people? Make no mistake, all of those things are important. But leaders often don't value people and relationships as much as they should.

It's ironic because what is the workplace, really? Sure, there are the facilities and the equipment and the goals and the numbers. But, really, a workplace is a coalition of people who have been brought together to accomplish something. Without the people, there is no organization. And yet, companies often act like the people are disposable.

Over the course of your career, you'll meet many people. Each of them will influence you in little ways, some of them in big ways. Every one of them has something to teach you, even if it's what *not* to do. As is the case with all relationships, professional relationships take work. And in our busy workdays, it's hard to fit in *another* thing. It's an investment, but it's well worth it.

Building relationships with and amongst your team will help them work together better, learn from one another, and make work more enjoyable. Even in this age where a lot of work is done remotely, people still seek connection. Valuing those relationships by putting time and effort into them should be a core focus for you as you develop your team.

Here's What to Do

Fostering relationships on your team doesn't have to be difficult. It starts with having the right people: people with good values who care about others. From there, it's all about creating the right environment. That means focusing on collaboration and making time for relationships. Here are two ideas for how to do that:

- **Don't compete; collaborate.** Many bosses encourage a lot of competition on their teams, thinking that the push will help them squeeze a little more profit or performance out of the group. The result is a team that is fractured, suspicious, and resentful. Being in constant competition is exhausting and pushes people needlessly into a distress state. At the end of the day, your team is going to be more successful if they work *together* instead of against each other.

- **Make time for relationships.** Making sure your team isn't overloaded is extremely important for growing meaningful relationships. When everyone is working in a frantic, haphazard way because they're trying to do more than is physically possible, they aren't going to spend time on relationships. They're more likely to be as transactional as possible, which will probably lead to disagreements and frustrations. You can play a central role as a connector—bringing people together, making introductions, and highlighting common interests.

Show your team that you truly value relationships by personally investing in them and giving them the time and space to do the same thing. This can (and should) extend outside of your team, crossing boundaries to establish and nurture relationships with other teams and more distant peers.

Take Action

If you're in the wrong mindset, you might think that spending time on relationships at work is a "waste of time." But it's actually one of the most important things you can do. Strong relationships build connection, and the ideas and results that come from collaboration are so much more than what any one person can achieve alone. Good relationships are the result of combining the right people with the right environment and showing them that you care.

72. Don't Let Disputes Fester

Help People Feel: *Respected*

Harmful Habit: *Resentment and Infighting*

Successful Strategy: *Direct Communication and Respect*

What's Gone Wrong

De-escalation is a rare skill, both in leadership and the general population. Which is curious because it is so desperately needed. We're working (and living) in a fast-paced, rather unforgivable world, where conflict is inevitable... especially in complex businesses where people both depend on each other and misunderstand each other *all the time.*

Because we work so quickly, we often don't take time to define things in crystal-clear, universally understood terms (if such a thing even exists). Instead, we rush ahead and make accidental assumptions that open the door to misunderstandings. No one intends for it to happen, but it does. Feelings get hurt; frustrations rise.

The real trouble can start when those feelings begin to fester, allowing toxic bad feelings to leech into your group dynamics. For example, if you have a development team that's understaffed and unable to deliver features that the sales team desperately needs in order to make their quotas, that's a recipe for disaster. On a smaller scale, you can have individual disputes (Frankie hates slow meetings, but Allesandra needs thoroughness). Or, on a global scale, cultural clashes can disrupt team dynamics. With diverse, geographically dispersed teams, these misunderstandings are bound to happen. No matter what caused the dustup, it's your job as team leader to de-escalate before things spiral any further.

Here's What to Do

It all comes back to empathy. Are your team members able to put themselves in each other's shoes? Do they even see the value in doing so? Without some guidance, perhaps not. That's where you come in.

It helps to start by separating the individuals involved so that they can have some time to process and express their feelings. In the case of our development team, they may feel that the sales team is asking for too much too fast (while the salespeople feel the engineers are being obstinate). Those feelings are valid, even if they were unintentionally caused. They deserve to be expressed in a safe and appropriate way.

Then ask the magic question, "Why do you think they did that?" It's designed to start the process of building empathy. You may get an angry answer at first ("Because they're idiots!"). That's okay (that's why you've separated them) as long as you can eventually get to a more realistic and empathetic answer ("Because they're understaffed.").

With the emotional prework done, try to bring the parties face to face so that you can moderate a healthy discussion and bring some understanding. If they're able to talk to each other and explain their perspectives, it helps. They can even potentially get to a place where they can work together to solve the problem. The salespeople may be able to select a feature that is their top priority so that the engineering team can deliver on that first. That's a much better situation than the perpetual rage that may have festered if the groups hadn't been able to actually talk to each other.

Take Action

The fast pace and high stakes of modern businesses are ideal conditions for conflict. These disputes usually aren't anyone's fault and they're bound to happen from time to time. Keep a keen eye out for the signs of frustration and carefully de-escalate the tensions before they become severe.

73. Teach Empathy Skills

Help People Feel: *Respected*

Harmful Habit: *Judgment and Fixed Thinking*

Successful Strategy: *Open Minds and Calm Perspective*

What's Gone Wrong

Empathy is one of the most important skills you can learn, both as a leader and a human. In business, it is the key to understanding your customers and being a good team member. When you can only see things from your perspective and feel your own feelings, you're unable to fully connect with the world around you. That kind of tunnel vision leads to selfishness, even if it's unintended.

Team dynamics are complicated. Each person on the team is busy and has their own values, preferences, and goals. Hopefully, each team member is self-aware enough to know what those are. Even better, it helps if they can clearly communicate them. But most people don't walk around with a name tag that says "I value my time above all else" or "Relationships are the reason I care about my work." It's going to take some empathy and effort to build those mutual understandings.

You should approach teaching empathy skills in the same way you would teach your team to communicate or prioritize—with specific techniques, continuous improvement, and some trial and error. This isn't commonly taught, but the potential benefits are worth the effort.

Here's What to Do

Developing empathy skills requires your team members to understand what others are feeling and why. There are many ways to improve your ability to do that, both intellectually and emotionally.

Intellectual empathy means leveraging what you know about someone to relate to them. This can be purely related to their work (What kinds of tasks do they do? What are their success measures?). It can also be more personal or preferential (What is their work schedule like? What are their hobbies?). Teach your team members that getting to know one another is time well spent. If you know that Nina has a photography class every Thursday evening, then you know not to ask her for "one quick thing" at 4:55 p.m. That knowledge helps a person to be more considerate and conscientious.

Emotional empathy involves understanding deeper feelings and motivations. These are felt more than known. Learning to pay attention to your colleagues' emotional cues is very valuable. Many people have been taught that they should keep emotion out of work, so there is a tendency to both hide and ignore emotion. But that isn't really possible—if someone is excited because they made a big sale or stressed because they're under a tight deadline, those are important emotions to understand.

The thing about empathy is that the more you use it, the more you have. So practice frequently and help your team do the same. Asking questions is a good way to guide someone into thinking more empathetically. Ask them to think about the other person's perspective and feelings. Show them that the misunderstanding or disappointment didn't happen for malicious reasons, but as a result of difficult circumstances (which should absolutely be true if you're hiring the right people on your team).

In a group setting, you can simply ask people to share:

○ What are your biggest concerns right now?

○ What made you choose this project?

○ What do you need from the rest of the team?

In one-on-one settings, the questions can be more direct. That's a more appropriate forum for asking a question like "What's bothering you?"

One of the most powerful questions to ask is "Why do you think they did that?" (the "they" usually being a colleague). If emotions are running high, you risk getting an answer like "because he's an idiot" or simply "I have no idea." But once things calm down, you can ask it more seriously. If something is running behind and one of your employees is getting increasingly frustrated, ask them if they know what's causing the delay. Encourage them to put themselves in the offending party's shoes and think about all of the contributing factors. That helps them explore both the intellectual (understanding what's happening and why) and emotional (understanding how others are feeling and what their experience is like). A little empathy goes a long way toward building stronger relationships, diffusing conflicts, and creating a more enjoyable work environment.

Take Action

Empathy is a powerful skill for both you and your employees. Teach your team to put themselves in others' shoes. What are they feeling? What are they dealing with? Help your team practice empathy and mutual understanding too, especially when there are disagreements or problems.

74. Institute a Shameless Policy

Help People Feel: *Safe*

Harmful Habit: *Any Form of Shaming*

Successful Strategy: *Collaborative Problem-Solving*

What's Gone Wrong

Have you heard of "blame-and-shame" leadership? Perhaps not. But you've *definitely* experienced it. Let's say Todd is a blame-and-shame leader. When something goes wrong, Todd follows a well-rehearsed, two-step routine:

1. Immediately demand to know who is to blame (and there *must* be someone to blame)
2. Angrily pontificate about the severity of the mistake

Why does Todd do this? Because it is *absolutely critical* that the mistake maker knows exactly what they did wrong and how serious it is. Todd is determined to shame them so thoroughly that they'll never deign to make a mistake again.

Oh, what did you say? We want people to feel comfortable admitting mistakes, asking for help, and learning from failure? Fine, fine. But Todd's still going to do the old two-step. That's okay, right?

No. It. Is. Not. This technique is disastrously counterproductive.

So why is this still happening? Unfortunately, shaming is a time-honored tradition, like underpaying employees and executives playing golf. It gives the shamer a sense of relief because they're distancing themselves from the problem. They believe it is normal—effective even—when it is actually causing massive harm.

Here's What to Do

In order to break this cycle, institute a Shameless Policy. This means that shaming is not allowed on your team. The shift is relatively straightforward. When a mistake is made:

- **Don't ask:** Who did this?
- **Do ask:** What should we do next?

It isn't that accountability isn't important. It's that the shaming is counterproductive. When someone makes a mistake, they already feel bad. They probably even already feel ashamed and are embarrassed to admit what happened. Exacerbating that feeling isn't going to help—it's just going to show every person on your team that, no matter their expertise or dedication, they're always one mistake away from ostracization.

Once you implement a Shameless Policy, everything becomes much more forward-looking. Shaming is all about looking back. While you want to learn from mistakes, you mostly want to focus on what to do next. That's what you want your team members to spend their time and brainpower on. If you can prove, through your behavior, that you aren't going to shame someone when they do something wrong, they can feel safe around you. You could even achieve that elusive state of "psychological safety" we all know we need.

And remember, the boss isn't the only potential shamer on the team. Anyone can be a blame and shamer. If it happens, redirect the culprit to the magic question "What should we do next?"

Take Action

Blame-and-shame behaviors are extremely common in the workplace. But, in order to build up your employees' confidence and help them focus on the future, redirect them to thinking about what to do next.

75. Shun a Litigious Mindset

Help People Feel: *Safe*

Harmful Habit: *Finger-Pointing and Accusations*

Successful Strategy: *Empathy and Good Faith*

What's Gone Wrong

People in the US have a strange fascination with law and order. Ever hear someone making legal threats over something completely trivial? There are two things that spur the "if I don't get what I want, I'll sue you" mindset: righteousness and black-and-white thinking. Let's break them down.

When someone feels wronged, it can trigger feelings of righteousness. Often, there is a layered set of circumstances that has caused the problem. But, when a person feels threatened, they're in a fight, flight, or freeze state, which can make it impossible to see those nuances and factors clearly. As a result, they jump to extremes.

As this mindset takes hold, things start to seem more black-and-white than normal. If the situation escalates, this makes it easy to jump from "I am right and you are wrong" to "you are wrong and you should be punished." That might look like this:

Behavior	Example
Reporting a person to their boss instead of speaking to them directly.	"He was late, and I want him to be written up!"
Making threats of serious consequences that are out of proportion with the situation.	"If you don't work on my project next, I am going to refuse to work with you again."
Claiming a breach of policy or process when the problem is more circumstantial.	"Our process document says this should be done in two days, but it has been three!"

If something serious has occurred, it should *absolutely* go through proper channels for review and action. However, much of the time these actions happen over regular interpersonal disputes and misunderstandings and don't require formal punishment, let alone legal action.

Here's What to Do

If you allow these litigious behaviors to fester and permeate your culture, you'll see issues like tattling, forming cliques, resentment, and infighting. Instead of letting misunderstandings spin out of control, use these de-escalation strategies.

Give Cooldown Time

Usually, the first thing that needs to happen is time to process emotions. The involved parties may be feeling angry, and therefore they need cooldown time. This doesn't need to be a lot of time, but give everyone a chance to take a break so that no one is acting in the heat of the moment.

Ask Questions

If one of your employees has fallen into the black-and-white thinking state, you may need to gently help them see other perspectives. Give them a chance to express how they feel, but also encourage them to focus on the problem, not the person. Good questions include: Why do you think this happened? What do you think we should do next? What would you do if you were the other person?

Bring People Together

After you give people time to calm down, it's important to bring them back together. Arbitrate a calm discussion between them, and offer help and support to find a solution together.

Take Action

When people feel wronged, they might make threats or accusations that are out of proportion with the situation at hand. If an accusation is serious, like harassment or discrimination, route it to proper channels immediately. However, if threats are being made over an unfortunate situation, like a missed deadline, take time to de-escalate the situation.

76. Take the Stigma Out of Failure

Help People Feel: *Safe*

Harmful Habit: *Fear of Failure*

Successful Strategy: *Learning from Mistakes*

What's Gone Wrong

Out of all of the trends that have passed through the business world in this century, the "fail fast" mindset from Eric Ries's *The Lean Startup* might be one of the best. We're all afraid of failure. It's scary and feelings of embarrassment are normal. But you can do a lot to take the stigma out of failure so that you and your team can actually *benefit* from failure.

Failure is a great teacher. Lots of ideas seem brilliant until you actually try them out. And it isn't just mechanical failures that matter. Some of the most important failures lie in how people responded to them. For example, you might have a product that is absolutely brilliant on paper. But if it doesn't excite people and if consumers don't actually want it, then it's a failure.

Human emotion isn't rational. It isn't supposed to be. There's an organic quality to our joys and desires that isn't supposed to be perfectly predictable.

Here's What to Do

Destigmatizing failure will require you to show some vulnerability and humility. When you do, it will be noticed by everyone around you. If you model those good behaviors, others will have the courage to do so too. Over time, the stigma will decay. What's left behind is a willingness, an eagerness, to fail and to learn.

The other key is reacting positively to the failures of others. When something doesn't go as planned, there is usually a natural trend toward punishment.

Show your team that you're much more interested in what was learned and what happens next.

Here are some appropriate responses that will put your team at ease:

O It's unfortunate that this first version didn't get the response we were hoping for. What do we want to try for version two?

O We knew that we were taking some risks here and not all of them paid off. What should we do next?

O I know that we're all disappointed in these results. It's okay to feel frustrated. Let's take some time to cool off before we try again.

O Even though this didn't work, we still moved forward. Now we can take these learnings with us as we try again.

It's important to acknowledge the failure out loud and state your feelings. If you're silent, your team may assume that you're quietly simmering with anger or judging them. Failure is a tool, and you want everyone to be comfortable using it.

Take Action

Sometimes you're going to fail and so will your team members. And that's okay. In fact, if you accept those failures with openness and humility, failure can save you from disastrous results. It can help you weed out the ideas that *sound* good from the ideas that are actually good. Be willing to experiment and encourage others to do the same.

77. Oust Bad Actors. Now.

Help People Feel: *Respected*

Harmful Habit: *Anyone Who Can't Meet Today's Behavior Standards*

Successful Strategy: *Safety and Respect*

What's Gone Wrong

What is a bad actor? We've all known different versions of this person throughout our careers. There's the righteous monster who takes out their aggression on everyone around them. There's the selfish freeloader who skates along without pulling their weight. And there's the two-faced liar who breeds distrust and panic. There are other versions too. Usually, everyone knows who the bad actor is. But they get a pass because they're brilliant (or special, or well connected). Every business is looking for that brilliant employee who's going to embody the best ideals and produce the best results. Brilliance is highly valuable—but it isn't the only thing that matters. While one person can have a lot of influence, no one person is as powerful as a team. So, if you have an employee that is a "bad actor," you need to remove them from your business. Now. These people will poison your team.

If your team contains bad actors, none of these other tips in this chapter are going to work. If you can't establish foundational safety, respect, and value on your team, a positive work culture simply isn't possible. Bad actors violate one or all of those basic tenants. They degrade safety, openly disrespect others, and don't value their teammates.

No one, no matter who they are or what work they're capable of producing, is worth the damage that is done to your team if those three tenants are sacrificed. You can give second chances, review specific behavioral examples, and do all of the responsible and respectful due diligence. If they cannot change, then they cannot stay. Ironically, these individuals are often protected or excused when that's exactly the wrong approach.

Here's What to Do

Once you're focused on what matters, you can let go of what doesn't. That means letting go of traditional power dynamics and hierarchies, giving you the freedom to directly address poor behavior. No one is untouchable. We've all seen what that has the potential to lead to—abuse, manipulation, and greed.

Managing bad behavior is one area where you should take a hard line. It's part of the tolerance paradox. While you seek to be tolerant and supportive, you cannot permit intolerance or unsupportive behavior on your team. You don't have to raise the guillotine on the very first misstep (that is, unless the behavior is actually harassment or discrimination, in which case immediate action is required). But, starting right now, don't permit bad behavior.

For example, if you have a very talented finance analyst on your team who is known for chewing out coworkers, decide now that you're not going to tolerate that behavior moving forward. Go to them directly and explain what is no longer acceptable and why. If it happens again, in a private setting, discuss their behavior and give them an official warning. Give them real opportunities to change, including access to education or support. But if they are unwilling, remove them from your organization.

Take Action

Bad behavior has been excused and ignored in businesses for far too long. No more. You can put a stop to it right now. Protect your team by refusing to allow inappropriate treatment, no matter who it comes from. Be clear and give an official warning so that the bad actor understands that you're serious. If the behavior continues, eliminate them and move on.

78. Let People Own Their Domain

Help People Feel: *Valued*

Harmful Habit: *Stifling Autonomy and Expertise*

Successful Strategy: *Confident Ownership and Teamwork*

What's Gone Wrong

How can a bad leader ruin a good team? By stealing their autonomy and stifling their spirit. In fact, when you come across a team that is miserable and disengaged, you can bet that lack of trust, lack of power, and lack of respect are going to be among their top complaints.

Weak leaders are insecure. Instead of trusting those around them, they continuously assert their dominance because they feel threatened. Weak leaders preside over weak teams, where only the leader is allowed autonomy and ownership and everyone else exists to serve the leader. This is the opposite of what you want. It doesn't allow for individuals or the team to achieve their full potential.

You want each person on your team to truly own their domain. If you have staffed the team appropriately, every person on it should have expertise in their area. You want them to feel confident and trusted enough to apply that expertise in their role. Instead of your team acting as an extension of the leader (who is limited to the knowledge and experience of a single person), you want them to work together and build on each other.

A team that works this way is always much more satisfied. No one wants to feel powerless and unheard, especially not the talented, hardworking people you want on your team. Make sure the team is diverse and open-minded so that they can learn from each other. Not only will everyone feel better, but their work will also be better by multitudes.

Here's What to Do

You're going to need to start all the way back at the hiring process. When a new role is needed, is it clearly defined? Do you know exactly what results are expected? Further, do you know how this role will operate within the team? With certain roles, like sales roles, that is usually pretty straightforward. They can be assigned specific accounts or a specific territory. With more matrixed roles, that can be more difficult. You may need to carve out the specific projects or responsibilities that this role will own.

Once you've appropriately structured and staffed the team, you need to build confidence and ownership. Remember, the benefit is that each person will feel more valued and you'll get better results. It's worth the extra effort it's going to take to get there. While new team members will need to learn operational processes, they also need early opportunities to contribute.

You should treat each team member like an internal consultant. Would you bring in an expensive consultant and then refuse to listen to them? Hopefully not (although it does happen, doesn't it?). Allow them to assess the situation, formulate a plan, put it into practice, and measure success. You're there to help people work together, secure resources, and guide the team forward.

Take Action

A strong team is one where everyone confidently owns their domain, listens and learns from each other, and is supported by a good leader. Building this type of team starts with clearly defined roles and real trust. If you can create those conditions, the result can be a high-functioning team where people can truly work together while applying their expertise.

79. Don't Try to Force Fun

Help People Feel: *Respected*

Harmful Habit: *Guilting People Into Obligatory Events*

Successful Strategy: *A Nonjudgmental Environment*

What's Gone Wrong

Shawna: *Hey Kelly. Are you coming to dinner with Jordan and me tonight?*

Kelly: *Sorry, I can't. It's company bowling night. Last time I skipped my boss told me that I needed to start being a "team player" if I wanted him to think I care about this job.*

Shawna: *Do you? Care about the job?*

Kelly: *Of course I do! My sales numbers are the best in our division! But god forbid I miss one cheesy work event and all of that hard work will pretty much become invisible.*

Poor Kelly. Do you think the goal of the company bowling outing was to make her feel inadequate? Because that's what it's currently doing.

Company parties and happy hours have been around forever. Sometimes they're enjoyable—however, they're often not. Frequently, they are activities that someone (usually the CEO or HR) thought would be fun and would be good "for culture."

But you can't make people feel better by just piling *more* onto their plates. That's what the "forced fun" does. Now, not only is there an insane amount to do, but people also have to show up after work and pretend to have fun.

You have to recognize the context of these events and how they look to your employees. For example, when you've been told that your reward for six consecutive weeks of overtime is two (small) slices of pizza, you can't help but feel annoyed and resentful. This is what people have been through. So when they get the calendar invite for these events, the dominant emotion is often stress.

Here's What to Do

Most importantly, you need to read the room. Too many bosses think only about what they enjoy and then thrust it on everyone else. Consider, for a moment, that you might be a little out of touch. Take your personal preferences and tuck them away for a moment.

Who is on your team? How do they want to engage? If you have a team of shy accountants, don't try to force them out of their shells. If they want to come out, they will. If your team is mostly very sociable and seems to have time for recreational activities, then start with something simple like Friday lunch outings, which can be done on company time, not personal time. Gauge their level of interest and react appropriately.

Next, stop judging. If someone doesn't want to participate, that should have absolutely no bearing on how you view them. Full stop. Because even if you think you know them or their type, there could be a multitude of reasons they don't want to or can't participate. They could be caring for a family member; maybe they volunteer. Or maybe they need more time to themselves. It doesn't matter. Absolutely none of those things affects their job performance. So check your biases and be careful not to judge someone for not loving this particular extracurricular activity.

Take Action

Forced fun isn't fun. It's actively demotivating. You are not entitled to someone's personal time nor are they obligated to enjoy the types of activities you enjoy. Tailor any extracurricular activities to the actual members of your team, taking their personalities and preferences into account. If they still aren't interested, chalk it up to your failure to understand them, not their failure to participate.

80. Calm the Generation Wars

Help People Feel: *Respected*

Harmful Habit: *Tension Between Generations*

Successful Strategy: *Mutual Respect and Cooperation*

What's Gone Wrong

If the headlines are to be believed, the generation wars are raging. The boomers hate the millennials, Gen Z isn't putting up with anyone's nonsense, and Gen X is silently judging everyone else while minding their own business.

While those (highly clichéd) statements are sometimes true, they also sometimes aren't. Yes, each generation has a distinct history and set of values. Yes, those values sometimes clash deeply and loudly. But it is also true that the workplace has space for all generations —because it has to. The workforce is composed of all generations. A healthy organization is going to ensure that the generations are tolerant of each other and, ideally, complement one another.

If that's going to be possible, then some of the natural tension between the generations needs to be calmed. That can be done with a foundation of empathy and respect.

Each generation has grown up in a completely different world. The resources, economies, technologies, and current events of each time period were different and distinct. That's important to remember when you're observing the differences in each generation's perspective and values. Here's a brief look at the events and technologies that shaped each generation as they came of age:

Generation	Boomers	Gen X	Millennials	Gen Z	Generation Alpha
Time Period	1946–1964	1965–1980	1981–1997	1998–2010	2011–Mid-2020s
Major Historical Events	Moon Landing (1969) Civil Rights Movement (1954–1968) Vietnam War (1955–1975)	Watergate (1972) Fall of the Berlin Wall (1989) The War on Drugs (1971)	9/11 (2001) Housing Crisis and Recession (2008) Repeal of "Don't Ask, Don't Tell" (2010)	COVID-19 Pandemic (2020) #MeToo Movement (2017) Black Lives Matter Movement (2013–Present)	COVID-19 Pandemic (2020) Ongoing events will continue to influence this generation. They will begin to enter the workforce in 2028.
Most Influential Technologies	Telephone Car and Air Travel	TV Computers	Internet Smartphones	Streaming Video Calling	TBD

Chart created from information at VisualCapitalist.com.

With these extremely different coming-of-age experiences, you can see how each generation was shaped differently. As with all diversity, there is a lot of value in that range of viewpoints.

Here's What to Do

The foundation for generational cooperation is respect. Here's what that means: All people from all generations are deserving of equal respect and treatment. Their perspectives are valid and important. This is not hierarchical respect, meaning that younger people are required to "respect their elders." They certainly shouldn't be asked to serve their elders either. It is important that everyone enjoys a universal respect, which at first may not feel comfortable to all generations. You want an even playing field where everyone is able to contribute as an individual.

Similarly, no one, in any generation, should be exploited in this system. That means that everyone should be fairly compensated for their work and experience.

If Hugo, twenty-four, has three years of experience and does mid-level work, he should not be treated like the office errand boy. In fact, unless you have an actual professional on staff who is paid for errand-like responsibilities, no one person should. You also can't allow age discrimination. If Terri, sixty-two, is tech savvy, her new software ideas should not be dismissed because she is viewed as "old."

If you can build a platform of universal respect, then the generations can learn from each other. Mentoring/reverse mentoring programs can be extremely powerful and beneficial for all participants. With good teamwork and humility, your team can benefit from every generation's perspective and experience.

Take Action

Generational diversity in the workforce is a powerful untapped resource. To benefit from it (and help your people do the same), establish foundational universal respect. Ensure that everyone is compensated and valued appropriately, and help them empathize with and learn from each other's diverse generational experiences.

part three

YOUR ORGANIZATION

Make Systemic Changes That Matter

If you are in a position to make or advocate for organizational change, you should do so. Very few people have that kind of access—don't waste it!

Recently, society has come to better understand the systems that surround and affect all people. We are all influenced by them and also trapped within them. This complicated situation is deeply interwoven with your workplace culture. You can't build a positive, healthy workplace on top of damaged, inequitable systems.

Making systemic change at your company is so important because, if you don't, you're likely to see the same problems crop up over and over again. It's tempting to think that serious problems are the result of just one person or mistake, but that's often not the case. If you take a step back, it's easier to see the bigger factors at play. Some of the elements you notice may be deeply entrenched both in your organization and in society at large. You'll have to work with many people to turn the tide—but never underestimate the power of people committed to change.

With so many complex, interrelated systems, it can be difficult to know where to begin—so difficult that you may be too intimidated to begin at all. That's where this part of the book comes in. Here, you'll find twenty ways to make important systemic changes, like addressing bias and reducing your carbon footprint. That includes ways to advocate for your team within the organization and how to modernize and advance your organization as a whole. These are significant projects that will require firm commitment and ongoing perseverance. As a result of your efforts, you'll see the biggest transformation and growth.

chapter 10

Advocate for Your Team Within the Company As a Whole

Your team doesn't exist in a vacuum; it is part of a system. Not only do you need to create a healthy environment within your team, but you also need to ensure that your team has a healthy place within the larger organization.

To do this, you need to be a good advocate for your team. Stand up for them, help them make connections, and ensure that they are respected and supported. Many modern businesses are siloed, not by design, but as a symptom of working at a fast pace within a complex organization. It's impossible for everyone to know everything that's going on, leading to feelings of frustration. Don't let your team suffer because of structural problems they didn't create.

In this chapter, you'll learn how to embrace your role as an advocate and live up to that responsibility. That means advocating for your team when dealing with managers of other teams, upper-level leaders, and more. The result will be a stronger appreciation for your team's efforts and easier access to necessary resources.

81. Don't Let Anyone Disrespect Your Team

Help People Feel: *Respected*
Harmful Habit: *Ego-Fueled Power Trips*
Successful Strategy: *Esteem, Respect, and Recognition*

What's Gone Wrong

Unless you're lucky enough to have built your business from the ground up, there are probably a few unpleasant personalities that you're going to have to deal with. They likely exist at or above your level, meaning that, while you can take a stand against them, you may not be able to remove them from the organization.

While you absolutely should not tolerate disrespectful or inappropriate behavior no matter who is perpetuating it, you'll also have to figure out how to protect your team if incidents happen that you couldn't prevent.

The modern workplace is built on collaboration and trust, not power plays. Regrettably, not everyone understands this, and so you still have people who want to figuratively flex their muscles and push people around. It makes them feel important. They're willing to tear others down if it makes them feel superior.

This behavior is usually a *learned* behavior. The perpetrator has almost certainly experienced this traumatic treatment and is reenacting the abuse consciously or unconsciously. But, no matter where it is coming from, this abuse is absolutely inappropriate. No one deserves this treatment.

Here's What to Do

You're going to need to fight this battle on two fronts:

1. **Be proactively vigilant.** Keep an eye out for any type of aggressive behavior. When you do see it, shut it down quickly.
2. **Listen carefully to what your team members say.** A person may behave acceptably when you're there, but act differently when you're not. If you're hearing complaints or stories, don't ignore them.

Here are three archetypes you're likely to have to deal with:

The Aggressor	The Complainer	The Joker
Is purposefully antagonistic and mean, openly insults others, and sees no need to respect anyone that is "beneath them."	Loudly voices disgust and judgment of others, is entitled and intolerant, blames people instead of recognizing difficult circumstances.	Makes inappropriate comments or microaggressions, claiming "It's just a joke," and disingenuously asking "Why doesn't anyone have a sense of humor anymore?"
How to Shut Them Down:	**How to Shut Them Down:**	**How to Shut Them Down:**
Don't permit them to work unsupervised with your team.	Don't engage with or encourage the complaining.	Don't play along.
Say "You will respect my people, or you won't work with them."	Ask "What would you do differently?"	Say "I don't see why that's funny. Can you explain it?"
Don't submit to their need for dominance.	Put them on the spot and ask for specific details or ideas.	Tell them that you will not listen to jokes made at your team member's expense.

If they refuse to stop, you may have to get HR involved. It's always best to address behavior directly. But if you've done that and the disrespectful behavior hasn't stopped, it may be necessary to escalate the situation.

Take Action

You can't have healthy, happy team members if someone outside of the group is behaving aggressively and disrespectfully toward them. No one, no matter who they are, should be allowed to treat your team (or anyone) in such a way. Keep an eye out for what is happening and what people are saying. Shut these tormentors down immediately.

82. Use Cross-Training to Build Empathy (and Relationships)

Help People Feel: *Respected*

Harmful Habit: *Siloed, Resentful Teams*

Successful Strategy: *Empathy and Functional Understanding*

What's Gone Wrong

Silos aren't just an organizational problem—they're actually endemic to modern working. The workplace has simply become too fast-paced and too complex for the average employee—regardless of status—to know *everything* that's going on in other departments.

The good news is that you have many opportunities to break down divisive barriers. If you want to prevent infighting and interdepartmental friction, then you need to get people out of their bubbles so that they can form relationships with people working in other areas. Some organizations are actually so big that even the most open-minded people can still get stuck in an "us versus them" mentality. When other people, roles, teams, and locations seem distant, they lose their humanity.

The result is that you start to lose sight of the fact that people you don't know are just as human as you are. They're busy. They're under pressure. They're facing personal and professional situations that are extremely demanding...just like you and your team. So, when an employee receives an assignment that isn't fully completed, their first thought is "Who screwed this up?" instead of "What happened here?" They're on the attack. This escalated annoyance is likely to put everyone on edge, and that's unproductive and, ultimately, toxic.

The key is positive proximity—in other words, getting different groups together in one way or another. Create opportunities for people from different teams to work together in a healthy, beneficial way. This doesn't have to mean physical proximity. In fact, it probably won't because most teams are at least partially dispersed. They just need a real chance to understand each other. Here are some programs that will allow crossover relationships to take root:

- **Cross-training:** Do accountants need to know about programming? Does HR need to know about sales? Absolutely. While it may seem like this kind of knowledge is "extra," it truly isn't. Your business will be more efficient and run more smoothly if people have a working knowledge of what others do and who they are. Let your team members teach others what they do, then let them learn from other departments.

- **Guest assignments:** If you've staffed your business appropriately (see #67: Be Honest about Workloads in Chapter 8), you should have leeway to free up team members to temporarily try other work outside of their department. Guest assignments can be structured or voluntary. Many businesses have very strong long-term guest assignment programs, where a person takes on a special role on a different team for 6–12 months.

- **Peer groups:** Peer groups can be led by a mentor or coach, or they can be led by the participants themselves. Ensure that the group has a clear purpose and is brought together by a common cause. That could mean that they're a committee that is working on a specific initiative, or it could be a learning group that is focused on a particular skill.

Each of these types of programs can be effective on their own. But they're even better when you do *all* of them. The network within your business is like a web. For each new connection formed, a person has access to (and empathy for) a whole new group of people. Make time for these programs and you'll have much happier workers that are more caring and collaborative.

Take Action

Your business will function better when people know and understand each other. Find structured, substantive ways to bring people together from across teams so that they can explain what they do, troubleshoot, and answer questions. If you make time for people to connect, it will allow them to establish relationships and exercise more empathy.

83. Build a Support Matrix

Help People Feel: *Safe*

Harmful Habit: *Siloed, Isolated Teams with Little Outside Support*

Successful Strategy: *Diverse, Wide-Ranging Forms of Support*

What's Gone Wrong

Even if you're the world's best boss, you're only one person. You can give your all to each one of your team members, but it really isn't enough. You can't always be there. Sometimes you won't have the right expertise to offer. Each person on your team deserves more. They deserve a proper support matrix. A support matrix means that a person has advocates, mentors, and partners in multiple directions. Ideally, some of that support will come from above, like a mentor from another team. Lateral support from peers or "buddies" is also important. It can even come from below through reverse mentoring programs or during cross-functional learning.

Today's organizations are heavily matrixed, meaning that there's interplay between various divisions, levels, teams, etc. The flatter structures mean that people are more accessible and, hopefully, that more information is shared between groups. This can be extremely beneficial for your people. It can offer more perspectives and, importantly, more connections. That's what's particularly beneficial about having matrixed support across the organization—it gives each person more opportunities to build beneficial relationships.

Here's What to Do

Ideally, you want to build support matrices at the organizational level. But, even if you can't, making cross-organization connections for your individual team is extremely helpful. Here are some forms that are worth exploring on a team level:

- **Onboarding buddies:** An assigned peer who will counsel a new employee during their onboarding period. While they'll get formal training elsewhere, this is someone that the new employee can turn to with more casual questions.

- **Peer groups/group coaching:** Groups that come together for either a functional or developmental purpose, like working on a special project or learning a specific skill. The group should meet regularly for two to three months so that they can get to know one another, share experiences, and work on a specific topic together. The group may be democratically led or run by an assigned coach or leader.

- **Mentors:** A leader (other than you) who shares their perspective and expertise. They can advise on career advancement, professional development, or other functional topics.

- **Sponsors:** A sponsor differs from a mentor in that they spend more time on advocacy and building professional connections. They focus on making introductions to other professionals who are influential or who have particular expertise.

- **Coaches:** Whether internal or external, coaches provide valuable support and can help a person through a time of career transition or growth. Coaches should help to develop specific goals and act as an accountability partner.

Imagine how beneficial it would be for people on your team to have these different types of support. Not only would your people gain tremendous knowledge, but they would also build relationships that could be extremely beneficial now and in the future. Even if you're not in a position to create programs like these, you can still make connections for individual team members.

Take Action

Everyone needs support. The more, the better. It takes a village, after all. There are many different forms of formal support that you can offer your team, each with a different purpose. Having a strong support matrix benefits each individual *and* it builds connection across the organization.

84. Take the Blame but Spread the Credit

Help People Feel: *Safe*

Harmful Habit: *Blame Dodging*

Successful Strategy: *Team Recognition*

What's Gone Wrong

Successes and failures elicit very different responses in the workplace, of course. Leaders are often quick to recognize their team's successes (hopefully also specifically recognizing the team members' amazing contributions). But failures happen. A team can have an extremely high success rate, but if they do make a mistake, everyone freaks out. Fingers are pointed; overreactions triggered. Leaders often contribute to this unfortunate dynamic, whether they realize it or not.

Businesses have been pushing the envelope on unrealistic work conditions for years. They push people harder, want them to work faster, get it done cheaper. This is the source of most of the preventable failures we see today. Often, it's only because of workers' extra effort that the mistake didn't happen earlier.

When the mistake does occur, everyone starts looking for the breakdown. But they fail to see the real culprit: the conditions themselves.

Here's What to Do

The single most important thing you can do to address this situation is to follow this mantra:

> *When something goes wrong, it's because of the leader.*
> *When something goes right, it's because of the team.*

This mantra will serve you well in your career. Let's look at it a little deeper.

Take the Blame

Your team is your responsibility. Everything that happens begins and ends with you. Not because you control everything (please don't), but because you're *responsible* for everything.

Let's look at some examples that prove this point:

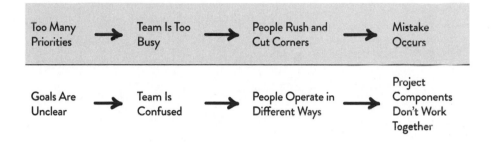

Usually, the "What Went Wrong" investigation starts with the third item in the chain: the cutting corners or operating differently. But no one follows the problem all the way upstream to the real root causes: There are too many priorities or goals are unclear. Surprise: Those are both failures of leadership. Take responsibility and focus on fixing those conditions so that the problem doesn't reoccur.

Spread the Credit

Most leaders don't do enough to celebrate successes in business. And they especially don't celebrate the individual contributions of the team members who made those successes happen. Often, there is an unspoken presumption that "that's their job." That reasoning doesn't negate the fact that it takes real, hard work to make success happen.

So, if a colleague comes up to you and congratulates you on a successful project, make sure you give recognition to the people who actually did the work. Explain, by name, who was involved and what they did. That sort of reputational boost can have a massive impact on someone's career, especially when you're telling someone with a lot of influence. They did the work, so make sure other leaders know about it. Even if you aren't asked, put your team members at the forefront of the conversation. Identify who had the idea, who carried it out, and how everyone contributed. Don't let your team members' efforts go unnoticed.

Take Action

In a healthy work environment, leaders take responsibility for mistakes and elevate others when they succeed. Just as poor planning or bad work conditions cannot be ignored, excellent performance should not go unrecognized. If something goes wrong and you see people starting to point fingers, pull everyone back and look for the root causes (hint: It might be your mistake). And, when something goes right, make sure that the people who made it happen are appropriately recognized for their contributions.

85. Be Serious about Safety

Help People Feel: *Safe*

Harmful Habit: *Bare-Minimum Safety Provisions*

Successful Strategy: *Proactive Safety Practices*

What's Gone Wrong

Some things are so fundamental that they should never be in question. Being safe at work is one of those things. Unfortunately, not all workplaces live up to that standard.

Safety is a wide-ranging topic. The government agency known as the Occupational Safety and Health Administration (OSHA) covers some core guidelines, like safe equipment use and protection from toxic chemicals. But some businesses have a way of skimping down to the bare minimum. They treat safety like an obligation, not a priority.

Sometimes you can see it in big ways, like organizations that have a safety violation or that allow their facilities to become run-down. But, more often, there are smaller, more subtle indications of neglect. The workers may be saying that something makes them feel unsafe, but no one listens. While people often associate OSHA and unsafe conditions with factory and laboratory workspaces, it's something *all* businesses need to worry about. Whether it's poorly lit parking lots, unshoveled entrances, or transmissible diseases that need attention—all companies need to ensure safety first and foremost.

This isn't an area where your commitment can waiver. If there's a hint of unsafe conditions, you should spring into action. You can't claim that safety is a top priority and then drag your feet when it actually needs to be addressed.

Here's What to Do

Here are some ways you as a team leader can actually make safety a top priority:

○ **Listen:** Safety isn't a label, it's a feeling. Your measure of workplace safety should include whether workers *feel* safe. Ask them how they feel. Allow them to provide anonymous feedback. When they do raise concerns, address them right away.

○ **Don't overwork people:** This is one of the most glaringly obvious ways businesses neglect safety. They schedule people for shifts that are far longer than are safe. Or they don't listen when people say they're exhausted. Don't push people past reasonable limits. They shouldn't have to tell you that twelve hours on the job is too many.

○ **Provide a range of safety options:** Not everyone's the same size, nor do they have the same preferences. If there are multiple types of protective equipment that are all equally protective, let employees choose what they want. They'll be more comfortable, which means they can focus on their work.

○ **Spare no expense:** Finally, if something is needed to improve safety, don't treat it like a budgetary burden. This is the last place for you to save money, not the first. Budget for contingencies. Research new safety options and stay informed of what they may cost so that you can plan appropriately.

Take Action

Safety should never be a question. It isn't a place to save money or to act slowly. Safety should be a top priority and your budget and actions should reflect that.

86. Promote from Within

Help People Feel: *Valued*

Harmful Habit: *Lazy, Haphazard Hiring*

Successful Strategy: *Ample Opportunities for Advancement*

What's Gone Wrong

Internal promotions will do amazing things for your organization. It's like a secret weapon that is deeply underutilized.

First, people who have worked their way up within your organization have experiences that outsiders don't. They've done the real work, so they have a much more realistic understanding of the business. That helps them to make estimates more quickly, know who to talk to in special situations, and hit the ground running. Even better, they're more likely to be respected because they've actually been there and know what they're talking about (assuming that they were good at their job—more on that in a minute).

The other major benefit is that promoting from within creates real, visible career advancement within your organization. Elite positions are already rare. If you're constantly filling them from the outside, then your people will feel like they're never going to have an opportunity to get promoted. When you actually move people up into meaningful leadership positions, they become a role model for others who are seeking to advance.

Are you sometimes going to have to hire from the outside? Maybe. If your company is in growth mode and is adding a lot of new positions, then it's very likely. But if your company is stable, then you should have a solid promotion pipeline built within your company. If not, it means that you aren't doing the necessary work to train and teach the people currently in your organization. External hiring can cover up the fact that you're not offering enough training and development, but it will leave your business brittle and disjointed.

Here's What to Do

Building a promotion pipeline takes effort and planning. In some ways, it's a numbers game. You need to invest in *lots* of people—as many as you have who want to learn and grow. Because when the time comes, you want them to be ready, and that isn't going to happen if you're not being proactive about it.

That means that you need to offer real leadership training. Leadership is a valuable set of skills that can be used by many people (not just managers). Project managers, team leads, technical experts, and others can all be leaders, even if they don't manage people at the present time.

What is good leadership training? Well, it includes many topics covered in this book. But, at the core, leadership is about people. You need to train your future leaders on how to develop and support others. That means skills like inclusion, empathy, and courage. Technical skills and traditional management skills are important too, so don't overlook them. You need well-rounded individuals who care about the right things.

Who should you be careful *not* to promote? The showy, power-hungry types that only want a promotion for themselves. If they're not in it to help others, then they're in it for the wrong reasons. They should spend most of their time supporting their team, not rubbing elbows with "important" executives. Unfortunately, these types have traditionally been very good at weaseling their way into powerful roles. Start a new trend now and hire the right people who can later work their way up the ladder.

Take Action

Promoting from within builds connection, authenticity, and expertise within your organization. It also provides meaningful advancement opportunities for your employees. To make it happen, you have to build a strong promotion pipeline of people who have healthy, well-rounded leadership skills. Invest in your people and they will grow alongside your organization.

87. Defend Your Team's Time

Help People Feel: *Respected*

Harmful Habit: *Taking On Any Project Someone Assigns Your Team*

Successful Strategy: *A Calm, Rational Decision-Making Process*

What's Gone Wrong

Some businesses are filled with so many squeaky wheels that they're practically a symphony of chaos. There's no real prioritization and so everyone is just shouting for attention and resources. Who gets stuck in the middle? The workers. They're the ones who have to deal with all of the whiplash requests and uncoordinated demands. Usually, no one steps in to protect them from the maelstrom.

Here's what usually happens: Someone with a lot of power, a lot of clout, or just a lot of gall has a "need." (We're using that term loosely here because, when you pressure test them, these needs usually fall apart.) Because the requester has power/clout/gall, everyone springs into action. They're told to be agile and so they react accordingly. This is how a couple of squeaky wheels can tank your productivity.

Has anyone even vetted this request? Has anyone analyzed how it fits into current priorities? Does anyone know the effort to output ratio? If you don't ask these questions, it's possible that no one will. You don't want your team subjected to rush projects that aren't actually useful *or* urgent.

Here's What to Do

When someone comes knocking with an unexpected demand, you need to vet the request rigorously. That doesn't mean that you need to be obstinate, but you should add a layer of examination that slows things down a bit.

Here are some questions to ask about the request:

○ Who needs this and why?

○ How will this impact the business?

○ Is the effort proportional to the output?

○ What is driving the timing?

○ What other stakeholders should analyze the request?

When you ask these questions, some red flags may emerge. If the answer to "Why do they need it?" is "because someone asked for it," the idea probably hasn't been properly evaluated. Pump the breaks and pull others into the process.

With a little extra analysis, a few things could happen:

1. **The request is accepted and made a priority:** If the request has true merit and will make a significant positive impact, pass it along to your team along with the answers you gathered. Other previously planned requests will need to be bumped out, which you can help manage.

2. **The request is accepted but not made a priority:** If the request has merit but it is not found to be truly time sensitive, you can add it to the priority list in the appropriate place. Instead of skipping the line, the requester can join it.

3. **The request is not accepted:** If you find that the request isn't going to make a significant difference or is duplicative/unnecessary, do not accept it. If the requester feels strongly, they can work to develop the idea further and come back with more research, preparation, and support.

Taking these steps before you dump a project on your team will show them that you value their time and talents—and you don't want to waste either resource.

Take Action

It is extremely refreshing to know that your boss isn't going to throw you curveballs all day long. If you're currently stuck in reaction mode and take anything given to you, try to be more stringent in your intake process. Don't accept requests that are haphazardly thrown together without proper preparation and analysis. If it isn't going to make a difference, don't do it.

88. Adopt a "Zero Interruptions" Policy

Help People Feel: *Respected*

Harmful Habit: *Rude Interrupters Who Overpower Others*

Successful Strategy: *A Safe Space for Everyone to Speak*

What's Gone Wrong

How can you expect people to feel heard if they aren't actually *being* heard? Because some of them aren't.

Being interrupted feels awful. Everyone deserves the opportunity to express their thoughts and share their experiences. When you're interrupted, the interrupter is telling you that they don't value your ideas and that they think their own thoughts are more worthy of expressing than yours. Often, that's done unconsciously. But the message is the same either way: I'm done listening to you.

Unsurprisingly, interruptions do not affect everyone equally. For example, according to a study at George Washington University, men interrupt women a full 33 percent more often than men interrupt other men. That single communication issue is enough to narrow the leadership pipeline for women. If women aren't being allowed to express their ideas as fully as men are, then they'll be viewed as having fewer ideas...which simply isn't true. And this isn't just a gender-based issue. Any time you have a perceived or actual power imbalance, you're likely to have more interruptions.

Interrupting, while generally not intended maliciously, has serious negative effects. It shouldn't be allowed to continue. So, it's time to get proactive either on a small or large scale.

Here's What to Do

Does your organization have any current communication standards? These are guidelines that communicate the expectations for communication within the company. Most do not. It may sound rudimentary, but something like a "Zero Interruptions" policy is a good place to start. Most people, when they are in a calm, logical state, will agree that no interruptions are beneficial. So, if you communicate that expectation proactively, then people will usually try their best to comply.

Here's how to roll out a Zero Interruptions stance to your team:

Communicate	Demonstrate	Moderate
Introduce the idea objectively (not as a reaction to current behavior).	Be careful not to interrupt. If you make a mistake, apologize.	If you see an interruption happen, politely moderate without judgment.
What It Sounds Like:	**What It Sounds Like:**	**What It Sounds Like:**
"I would like to introduce a Zero Interruptions policy on this team so that everyone can fully express their ideas."	[Silence] Or "I'm sorry, Tori. I had an idea and I got overexcited. Please continue with your explanation."	"Marc, I know you didn't intend to interrupt. Could you please allow Malia to continue?"

But, you may ask, what if someone is too long-winded? Don't you have to interrupt them so that they don't completely dominate the conversation? Possibly. However, try to address that as private feedback first. Let them know that you value their ideas, but that they should be conscientious of leaving time for others to share. If they are still struggling, it would be better to try a nonverbal signal—like tapping the table—as a gentle, private reminder to wrap it up.

Take Action

Some people, particularly those who already have more disadvantages in the workplace, are much more likely to be interrupted than others. To combat this, implement a "Zero Interruptions" policy. Be careful to introduce the idea proactively and not in reaction to anyone's specific behaviors. If you do have frequent interrupters or conversation dominators, give them that feedback privately.

89. Take Harassment and Bullying Complaints Seriously

Help People Feel: *Safe*

Harmful Habit: *People Who Are Inappropriate or Disrespectful*

Successful Strategy: *A Safe Workspace That Protects People*

What's Gone Wrong

Despite the fact that we know that harassment is underreported, and despite movements like #MeToo, victims are still usually met with skepticism and aggression when they come forward. They are asked to tell their story—however traumatic it may be—over and over again so that doubters can attempt to poke holes in it. They may be labeled "difficult." We offer them virtually no protection—certainly not enough to balance out the massive systems they're going to have to navigate as they attempt to find safety.

For many people, victims are threatening. There are too many painful truths to accept in their stories, and so they distance themselves to push the pain away. They're willing to discredit and undermine the victim if it means that they don't have to accept the horrible things that happened to them. All of that denial is, sadly, deeply woven into current views of harassment.

Bullying, while not as well examined as harassment in adult settings, is also poorly handled when it is reported. There could be learned behavior at play—people who endured some form of bullying during their careers might be hesitant to help. According to a 2011 study published in *Semantic Scholar*, they may instead perpetuate the bad behavior by either normalizing it or by carrying it out themselves.

For too long, companies have failed to take these complaints seriously. The behavior hasn't gone away on its own. We need to meet it head-on and make the workplace safe for everyone.

Here's What to Do

If you receive a report of harassment or bullying, recognize that, as a person of power, you have a moral (if not legal) responsibility to help. That report may come to you directly from the victim or it may come from witnesses. Either way, you need to support the victim and ensure that everyone knows that these behaviors are unacceptable and will not be tolerated.

Start by investigating the claim according to company guidelines. You should take it seriously, but be conscious of your own safety and mental health. Depending on your role, you may need to bring in other leaders or HR representatives. Do that if you need to, but recognize that it doesn't mean your role is over. Often, victims are passed off to people who then block or discourage them in the reporting process. Anyone on your team will need your ongoing support, especially if it means standing up to powerful company figures.

Be careful to keep the blame in the correct place: on the bully or harasser, not the victim. Victim blaming is a frequent mistake. If excuses are given, consider them carefully and critically. And throughout the process, make sure to offer support and safety. Usually, everyone is eager to claim that problems are fixed, even when they aren't.

Sometimes, the harasser or bully is going to need to be removed from the company. If their behavior warrants immediate removal, don't delay. You have to show them and your organization that there is no place for harassment and bullying in the modern workforce. If the behavior isn't so severe that it warrants immediate termination, give the person the chance to understand their mistake and correct their behavior. But if they get to three strikes, they're out. That might mean you lose a talented team member, but their talent and power do not give them permission to treat others terribly. Do not make exceptions for anyone whose behavior is inappropriate.

Take Action

Harassment and bullying have no place anywhere, including your company. Even if these behaviors were widespread in the past, they cannot be tolerated today. If you receive a report, support the victim and persistently address the issue until everyone can truly feel safe and welcome.

90. Accept Losing the Ones You Love

Help People Feel: *Safe*

Harmful Habit: *Trapping Employees or Retaliating Against Them If They Try to Leave*

Successful Strategy: *A Welcoming, Supportive Environment Where Each Person Can Pursue Success*

What's Gone Wrong

If you're lucky, you'll have the opportunity to lead some outstanding team members over the course of your career. Some will be exceptional (you do know how to hire a great team, after all). Others will amaze you with their talent or drive. You might wish that these stars could stay on your team forever...but that just isn't going to happen. Sometimes you have to accept that your best people may be ready to move on. Sometimes you have to lose the ones you love.

For some, the thought of giving a current employee a reference is blasphemy. They will stomp their feet and throw a tantrum every time someone dares to leave. That is childish and ignorant. When a bad boss finds out that an employee is thinking of leaving, they suddenly morph into a crazy ex who is desperate to dump you before you dump them. Again, this is petty, insolent behavior, but it is *common*. Have you ever worn a particularly nice outfit to the office and had your boss rush up and ask you if you had a job interview? The paranoia and corresponding hysteria have resulted in firings, abuse, and other forms of retaliation.

If you truly care about your people, you should *celebrate* it if they find a great opportunity elsewhere. If you have a data analyst who doesn't have the opportunity to use their full set of skills at your company, would you really want them to decline an offer from a tech powerhouse? If you've tried to get someone a salary adjustment but HR is blocking it, do you actually want them to continue earning below their potential? If the answer is yes—or even "it depends"—please take a good look in the mirror. Everyone deserves to find the best path available to them.

Here's What to Do

It's important to be open and honest with your team members. Make sure they know that you support them and want the best for them, unconditionally. Remember, they may have had past bosses who were mean to them when they left, so they may not share much information unless they're sure they can trust you.

Be liberal with your recommendations, introductions, and mentorship. If you know a company or a position that would be a better fit for one of your team members, don't gatekeep. You certainly don't want to actively push your talented employees out the door. But you do want to be realistic and supportive of your team members' success, even when that means they move on.

Take Action

If you want to create a safe, healthy environment on your team, then you don't want anyone to feel trapped in their job. Be a boss who genuinely cares about your team members and their success. If there are better opportunities available—or if it's just time for someone to go—be a positive part of that transition.

chapter 11

Make Systemic Changes

When you really want to make a difference, you have to start at the top. You have to go to the highest level to break down broken systems and replace them with healthy ones. This work isn't easy and it can take a lot of time, but it's well worth the effort when you consider the safety, respect, and value it brings your employees.

While it would be great to wave a magic wand and eliminate racism or bullying, that's obviously not realistic. Still, taking specific concrete actions can make a difference. While the ideas in this chapter are system-level changes, they can start at the "local" level. If you're able to incorporate them into your company's policies, great—they will benefit your entire organization. If that's not possible yet, though, you can still do each of these on your own team and it will make a difference.

In this chapter, each item has a practical, achievable starting point that will address a larger, systemic problem. In the end, the final two topics— #99: Prioritize the Greater Good and #100: Value People over Profits—are rules you can live by. If you do, it won't matter what scale you're working on, you'll still make an incredible difference.

91. Stand for Something

Help People Feel: *Respected*

Harmful Habit: *False Promises and Insincere Values*

Successful Strategy: *Personal and Professional Integrity*

What's Gone Wrong

We are entering an age of great responsibility. We have a lot of work to do to make the world a better place, but we also have more knowledge, more transparency, and more reach than ever before. You get to decide if you're going to pick up this mantle. Are you going to betray yourself and your values just because "this is the way we've always done it"? Or are you going to be true to yourself and stand up for what you know is right?

You might think that business isn't the place for you to live your values. But, in truth, businesses are some of the most powerful entities on the planet. While they sometimes (rightfully) get put in check, their priorities usually become the world's priorities. Because of their spending power, businesses have huge opportunities to influence culture. On a smaller scale, they also impact their employees' day-to-day lives. They are massive forces that can have either a positive impact or a negative impact.

When businesses have a positive impact, the world becomes more equitable, sustainable, ethical, and healthy. When they have a negative impact, the opposite happens. As a leader, you want to make sure you're helping your company stay on the positive side.

Here's What to Do

There is often a lot of pressure to ignore your values in service of the business, but doing so is clearly wrong. And now that business practices are more transparent and out in the open, you can get called out if you allow injustices on your watch. With that in mind, here are three things to look at in a new light:

- **Precedents:** Just because a process is "the way we've always done it" doesn't make it right. After all, precedent indicates that certain people should make less money than others, businesses can take advantage of workers, and it's all right to prioritize profit over people. But all of those things are deeply wrong. Choose to reject unjust precedents.

- **Unintended consequences:** No one intends for negative consequences to happen, but they do. Manufacturing causes pollution. Bias causes inequity. Usually, these actions aren't done intentionally, but that doesn't negate their impact. Don't ignore negative consequences just because they're unintentional. Dissect them, find the root cause, and make it right.

- **Centering:** Who is at the center of your conversations and practices? Is it the people who already hold a lot of power? Or is it less powerful people who need your help? Often, there is a de facto centering of C-level executives and shareholders. Their needs are considered to be the most important because they hold the purse strings. But are they actually most important? Do they need you the most? Consider how you can recenter in a way that is more merited.

Take Action

As the saying goes, if you don't stand for something, you'll fall for anything. We've been conditioned to ignore that idea at work so that we can prioritize profit and productivity above all else. As a leader, you can change that. You have influence. Reconsider what's going on around you and ask yourself whether it is truly right.

92. Differentiate Systemic Problems

Help People Feel: *Safe*

Harmful Habit: *Blowing Isolated Problems Out of Proportion*

Successful Strategy: *Addressing Systemic Problems Directly*

What's Gone Wrong

Not all problems are created equal. In fact, some problems are actually distractions that simply aren't worth your time. If you give credence to the wrong problems, you waste everyone's time.

Learning from mistakes (or even unexpected results) is invaluable. In fact, with the level of competition organizations face today, learning from mistakes and adapting quickly is essential for survival. But it's important that you take the right lessons from each situation.

The difference between a systemic problem and an isolated problem is whether it is likely to happen again. It's critical that you differentiate between the two:

○ **Isolated problems** are largely unpredictable. There are so many prospective isolated problems that you can't possibly prepare for them all. It's a fool's errand to try.

○ Conversely, **systemic problems** *are* likely to repeat. They come from a specific cause, like understaffing or process gaps. You can't ignore or fail to prepare for these—if you do, you're setting yourself up for disaster.

Both types of problems have consequences, but you're better off focusing your energies on systemic problems.

Here's What to Do

The good news is once you differentiate between systemic and isolated prob lems, you can react to them accordingly. Here are some examples:

	Systemic Problem	Isolated Problem
Definition	Likely to happen again.	Specific to a project, situation, team, or person.
How to Address It	Deconstruct the problem, identify the root causes, and implement concrete changes.	Acknowledge the problem, ensure that it is well understood, and move on.

Let's look at an example. Imagine that you run a team of eight people. One of them falls suddenly and seriously ill with an unexpected condition and needs to take a four-week leave of absence. Their work must suddenly be reallocated, which is distressing for everyone involved. Now, this example may illuminate some systemic problems. For example, let's say there was no available project documentation that outlined the status of the ill employee's work. But the problem of their leave of absence is likely to be an isolated problem, especially on a team of only eight people.

This situation has presented two problems: project documentation (systemic) and sudden leaves of absence (isolated). Which one should you spend more time on? The issue of project documentation. Dive in; figure out why you have this gap and how you can address it. Are there good documentation tools available to your team? Are documentation requirements well defined? Is time allotted for people to properly document? Investigate and make timely changes.

Take Action

Reflecting on mistakes is important for all organizations, not to take someone to task but to learn what went wrong. While some problems are worthy of significant time, others are not. Don't waste time building solutions for situations that are unlikely to recur. Instead, differentiate systemic problems and be sure to dedicate real time to them so that they can be properly addressed. Once you understand the root causes, implement real, concrete changes to address them.

93. Combat Bias

Help People Feel: *Safe*

Harmful Habit: *Bias Denial*

Successful Strategy: *Humility and Learning*

What's Gone Wrong

Bias is part of our world. No one has escaped it unaffected. Instead of ignoring bias, you need to acknowledge its presence and then actively combat it. This is an area where it's hard to put out the fire from inside the house.

You may think that you (or your team) don't need formal bias education, but you do. Education is very powerful in this area. The issue with bias is that many people are unaware of their biases and then become defensive about them if any are called out. Facing this type of challenge isn't done overnight and needs repeated education and support. So many businesses have pledged to "do better." But if yours isn't currently taking action, you're not following through on those promises.

Here's What to Do

The first step is admitting you have a problem (as it usually is). At minimum, there should be open and frequent conversations among your leadership team about bias and what should be done about it. For the more concrete items, data is helpful. What are your race and gender breakdowns? How is your LGBTQIA+ representation, if known? What do the employee engagement surveys say about belonging and inclusion? Data can help you get out of the trap of discussing whether there is a problem (there is) and get your colleagues focused on what to do about it.

If your leadership team has done the work and confronted bias within themselves and their ranks, then spread out to the wider organization. Raise awareness about bias. Give practical examples. Share your action plan and give updates on how it is going. It's very likely that you may need some outside support. If you are part of a large organization, then you should have a head of Equity, Diversity, and Inclusion. Is their department well funded? Would they like to bring in outside educators or coaches to support their work? Or to support people who may be more disadvantaged?

If you discover more serious bias issues in this process, additional action is needed. If you have bad actors, they cannot be allowed to continue those behaviors (and if they cannot change, then they have to go). If your representation isn't up to a current standard, don't just hope that it will get better eventually. Consult with experts on how to fix the problem (yes, it is a problem) and then follow through. If you want your business to survive into the next era, this isn't optional. The public demands it. Lead the way instead of lagging behind.

Take Action

Businesses have promised the public that they are going to do more to combat racism, sexism, and xenophobia of all kinds. To deliver on those promises, you need to invest. Educate and explore within your leadership team and across the organization. Your good intentions show that your heart is in the right place, so seek out the programming you need to put your business on the right track.

94. Check Your Carbon Footprint

Help People Feel: *Safe*

Harmful Habit: *Ignorance of Your Company's Ecological Impact*

Successful Strategy: *Ecological Responsibility*

What's Gone Wrong

No one is untouched by global climate change, which is helping to cause more extreme wildfires, hurricanes, and droughts. Businesses are powerful and influential parts of society. When large corporations take a stand on an issue, change is more likely to happen.

Here are some of the ways businesses impact climate change:

○ **Procurement:** Depending on your methods of procurement, your business may directly or indirectly contribute to carbon emissions. It is important to understand where your goods and services come from and how they are obtained. If you obtain large quantities of good or services from third-party vendors, find out how their procurement processes work.

○ **Manufacturing:** When we think about corporate carbon emissions, we often think of the manufacturing process. While it is not the only contributor, it certainly can be a major source of problems. Businesses may continue to rely on harmful practices because of either cost or capability.

○ **Shipping:** The transportation of goods is another major contributor, especially considering our global economy. It doesn't help that customers expect to receive their orders almost instantaneously. As with procurement, you will need to know what your shipping partners are doing to reduce or control carbon emissions.

○ **Travel:** Especially now that most teams are dispersed, it's nice to get everyone together occasionally. But it is important to temper the need for in-person presence with ecological responsibility. Virtual tools are now ubiquitous, so they should be used liberally.

○ **Facilities:** Finally, your facilities are energy consumers and thus, carbon emitters. Not only do you need to examine how your facilities are powered, but you also need to know how they're constructed. Some businesses are seeking to achieve LEED (Leadership in Energy and Environmental Design) certification for their facilities, which takes into account factors like location and commute accessibility.

Here's What to Do

Corporations have the power to either actively exacerbate climate change or actively counter it. It starts by understanding your company's current carbon footprint, as described in the previous section. There are excellent tools publicly available on sites like Watershed.com or Berkeley.edu that will walk you through a thorough carbon footprint assessment. It may seem daunting, but it's possible that your business is doing more harm than you even realize. If you're feeling overwhelmed, you could even reach out to an organization like Greenly, which specializes in assisting businesses with their carbon footprint.

Striving to achieve carbon neutrality is a good place to start. If you need a little inspiration, it might surprise you to learn that Formula 1 has committed to become carbon net zero by 2030, and Amazon has committed to reach net-zero carbon emissions by 2040. Businesses don't always achieve those goals, so they should be taken with a grain of salt. But making a serious, public commitment *is* a step in the right direction.

Take Action

Whether you like it or not, your business is a direct contributor to climate change. All organizations, especially large businesses, hold the power to affect climate change. Make sure you know your organization's carbon footprint. Push for concrete, public goals to become carbon neutral or carbon negative.

95. Remove Degrees from Your Job Requirements

Help People Feel: *Safe*

Harmful Habit: *Artificial Requirements That Promote Exclusivity*

Successful Strategy: *Open-Minded Recognition of Skills, Experiences, and Abilities*

What's Gone Wrong

A few years ago, it became a ubiquitous joke that most entry-level jobs seemed to require five years of experience (and a master's degree!). Um...why?

Jobs and the workplace have changed so much that old predictors of success are much less likely to be accurate. For example, college degrees do not actually predict job success. Want to know what they do predict? Socioeconomic background. Whiteness. Privilege. Exactly what businesses *don't* want as they attempt to diversify.

College degrees continue to become more and more expensive. It's a multibillion-dollar industry based on asking young adults to take out massive loans they can't afford. A college education is a beautiful thing—but, right now, they're structured like luxuries. Will they make a candidate knowledgeable, well connected, and well rounded? Yes. Is that the *only* way to become those things? No. Education and information are more accessible than any time in history. The main difference between people who go to college and those who don't is whether they can afford it.

Including strict degree requirements in job descriptions makes businesses complicit in this entire system. We're telling kids that the only way to be successful is to graduate from an expensive college. It's simply untrue.

Businesses often say without any thought that degrees are necessary, which is, frankly, old-fashioned thinking. In doing so, they continue to hinder upward mobility for People of Color, people from rural areas, and others from disadvantaged backgrounds.

Here's What to Do

Go take a look at your job descriptions. Look at each one and ask yourself to truthfully answer this question: Do these jobs actually require degrees? Some jobs do: accountants, nurses....Those are jobs where people actually learn to do them in school. Likewise, if there are certifications or other alternative forms of formal education that apply to the position, they're fine to include.

However, the vast majority of corporate jobs are more removed from their related degrees (that is, if there even are degrees that are truly related). Here are some jobs that do not require degrees:

- Project Manager
- Social Media Manager
- Business Development Representative
- Product Manager
- Data Entry Specialist
- Customer Service Representative
- Recruiter
- Graphic Designer
- Software Developer

Would a degree benefit people in these roles? Yes. But that is not the only way to gain the knowledge and experience to do them well. So there is no reason to *require* them.

Remove the degree requirements from as many job descriptions as you possibly can. When you do, you're giving yourself immediate access to a more diverse group of candidates. Refocus your screening and interview processes on skills, experience, and achievements.

Take Action

Look through all of your job descriptions and remove the degree requirements from as many as you can. If a degree is truly required for a role (think: chemist), then keep it. If it's not, then cut it. You'll gain access to a wider pool of more diverse candidates, and you'll positively contribute to making good jobs accessible to more people.

96. Decode "Fit"

Help People Feel: *Safe*

Harmful Habit: *Homogenous, Intolerant, and Unwelcoming Biases*

Successful Strategy: *Clear, but Inclusive, Values*

What's Gone Wrong

Like so many corporate buzzwords, "fit" can mean many things depending on the situation. Your boss has a problem with Elizabeth? Suddenly she's no longer a *good fit*. HR prefers one qualified candidate over another? Again, they're quick to claim fit as the reason.

When "fit" is used as a euphemism for personal preferences, that's one thing. But it becomes much more dangerous when it's used—often unintentionally—as a front for bias.

The idea behind cultural fit seems good on the surface: If an organization has properly defined its values and expectations, then it can communicate them to current and prospective team members. That is great for making sure everyone is on the same page. The problem is that assessing whether someone is a match for a team can unintentionally lead people to pick more people who look and sound like them, and then, by extension, you've got bias.

For example, even if a company values boldness, is there room for someone that is quiet and thoughtful? Or, if a company values "professionalism" (see #10: Be "Unprofessional" in Chapter 1), can that be used as an excuse to exclude People of Color, members of the LGBTQIA+ community, or others? We've all probably seen times when a person who speaks differently or has an alternative hairstyle is immediately put in the "maybe" or "no" pile. That's where the decoding needs to happen. Brightly colored hair is likely not stopping this person from performing their job well. Unfortunately, companies often hide behind "fit" when they really mean "not like us."

Here's What to Do

Examine your company culture carefully and with an open mind. Cultures aren't set in stone—they are constantly evolving as people enter and exit the business and as society and the marketplace change. That evolution is good. It means that you can allow for growth and learning.

If a company values innovation, for example, people should be allowed to express that in different ways. You *don't* want a team that's dominated by one personality type. When you think of innovation, certain styles may come to mind—someone who is outspoken, unconventional, and mischievous. But that is not the only way to be innovative. You could innovate by being analytical or out of a desire for simplicity. That's how innovation can be inclusive.

Some values, however, may not be inclusive. As mentioned, "professional" is code for white, cisgender, and heterosexual people. Values like friendly, respectful, well spoken, dedicated, and tough must be thoroughly scrutinized to see if they are being (or could be) used to exclude People of Color, women, LGBTQIA+ individuals, people with a disability, neurodiverse candidates, or anyone who is considered "different." Ask yourself: Could this value be considered code for something else? Could someone, purposefully or unintentionally, use this as a rationale for exclusion? If so, eliminate it and focus on the skills, abilities, and experiences that create the culture you really want.

Take Action

Cultural "fit" can be a dangerous idea if it is used as code for bias. While often unintentional, certain values may be coded to exclude People of Color, women, LGBTQIA+ individuals, people with disabilities, or others. You should carefully examine all of your values and hiring criteria to see if they are exclusive or inclusive.

97.   Welcome Gen Z

Help People Feel: *Respected*
Harmful Habit: *Bias Against Young People*
Successful Strategy: *A Welcoming, Supportive Workplace*

What's Gone Wrong

When a new generation enters the workforce, the "establishment" has a collective freak-out. And it lasts about as long as it takes for another new generation to come along. It happened with Generation X, it was absolutely rampant with millennials, and now Gen Z (those born between 1998 and 2010) is in the hot seat.

Gen Z is the most diverse and well-educated generation ever to enter the workforce. They are also coming of age at a time when there is more opportunity than ever. So they have an abundance of options, a bold view on the world, and they're still young enough that their financial constraints are limited (although student loans continue to be a major problem).

As a result, they are comfortable standing up for their values, speaking their minds, and leaving if they aren't being treated well. That's different from Gen X and millennials, who were told "that's just the way it is, so get used to it."

Here's the thing: Companies should *want* to hire people who aren't afraid to stand up for themselves and do what's right. Gen Z is exactly what the workforce needs. So use your power as a leader to welcome them with open arms and allow them to pull the world in a more responsible, respectful direction.

Here's What to Do

If you want to successfully recruit and retain Gen Z professionals, you're going to have to work for it. Gen Z has been marketed to extremely heavily, so they're savvy. If it's not real, they're not interested. With millennials, organizations threw

LaCroix sparkling waters in the office fridge, loosened the dress code, and continued with business as usual. That's not going to work anymore. Instead, listen to what is important to them and provide those things in real, substantive ways.

In 2022, Handshake asked Gen Z workers what they wanted from their jobs. Here's what they said:

Percent	Factor	So You Need To Have...
70%	Pay or Compensation	Generous pay practices and pay transparency
67%	Ability to Advance in Their Career	Many career pathways, accelerated advancement opportunities, and continuous professional development
66%	Employee Benefits	Low-cost, high-coverage plans that include good mental health coverage
61%	Having Fun at Their Job	A healthy, happy work environment and ability to build community (even remotely)
55%	Commitment to Diversity, Equity, Inclusion, and Belonging	Equitable representation, excellent support, and a track record of real action
50%	Commitment to Sustainability	An environmental sustainability plan with hard data and firm deadlines

Source: Handshake.

As you can see, these factors can't be faked. Authenticity and commitment are extremely important in showing that you're serious. If you make empty promises and then don't follow through, don't expect a second chance. Gen Z has the freedom to move on as quickly and as frequently as they want.

Take Action

Organizations need Gen Z (probably more than Gen Z needs them). Don't waste time grumbling about their unwillingness to put up with corporate shenanigans. Instead, get to work proving that you put your money where your mouth is. Pay attention to what this generation wants, and get serious about providing it.

98. Don't Be Top-Heavy

Help People Feel: *Valued*

Harmful Habit: *Bloated Executive Teams*

Successful Strategy: *A Balanced Workforce of Doers*

What's Gone Wrong

What happens when you have too many captains and not enough sailors? Well, your ship probably doesn't go anywhere. And there's probably a lot of infighting and power grabbing happening on the bridge of this sinking ship.

That general scenario describes a lot of workplaces, doesn't it? There's a fleet of feisty executives rushing around, vying for power, with very few people (certainly nowhere near enough) to actually run the place. What's the executive solution to this staffing problem? More executives, of course!

Nope. Top-heavy organizations often topple under their own weight. The problem is that ego prevents out-of-touch "leaders" from seeing what's really going on. They're happy to pay hundreds of thousands of dollars to bring on another executive that will lead a "Center of Excellence," but they refuse to shell out another $2/hour for low-wage workers. Because they think higher-ups are worth it, but that people who are actually doing all of the work…aren't.

Avoiding this fate takes some careful thought and real labor planning. You need to get to know your business very closely so you are well aware of everyone's contribution to the whole. You're not just looking for "fat" to trim, you're looking to properly allocate compensation budget and recruiting resources.

Here's What to Do

Labor planning isn't a one-time thing. Until fairly recently, it was an annual process. But not anymore. Now it's a continuous cycle:

Understand the Work

You must have a real understanding of what the work is, what skills are needed to do it, how much time it takes, and what the challenges are.

Be Realistic

Know how much work you plan to produce in the next 6–18 months. How many person-hours are needed? Be sure to base this on real time frames, not estimates. You need real numbers, not the numbers you wish you could have.

Use Good Data

You can't staff for "best-case scenarios." You have to factor in PTO, maternity leaves, training time, internal promotions, etc. In short, you should staff slightly more than you think you need so that you have coverage.

but also...

Most executives have been approaching labor planning backward. Instead of staffing for what they want to get done, they are constantly hunting for where they can make cuts. Think about it this way: Companies almost always rehire for empty top-level positions, unlike lower-level jobs, which often disappear when someone leaves. That's why you need to check both the top and the bottom levels of your organization to be sure they are staffed appropriately and proportionally.

Take Action

You have big goals for your organization. To make those happen, you need good leadership, but you also need a strong workforce to match. If you understaff, it won't matter how many incentives you offer, you're going to struggle. Everyone will. Appropriately plan for a labor force that matches your goals.

99. Prioritize the Greater Good

Help People Feel: *Respected*

Harmful Habit: *Doing Harm, Even Inadvertently*

Successful Strategy: *Doing Good*

What's Gone Wrong

prioritize *(verb) pri•or•i•tize: to designate something as more important than other things.*

Why is there a dictionary definition for a very basic word here? Because everyone seems to have forgotten what it means. If a project is deemed a priority, but so is every other project, then it isn't a priority. How many times have you heard "This isn't the highest priority...but it still has to get done"? If you can't successfully deprioritize, then you haven't actually prioritized anything either.

A lack of this skill is why prioritizing the greater good often gets lost in the shuffle. Ask any business owner and they will tell you that they do, in fact, prioritize the greater good—but their actions usually say otherwise. That's because they refuse to deprioritize any of their current business practices.

Take carbon emissions as an example. We all know it's in our best interest to reduce carbon emissions, but the list of excuses companies offer of why they can't hit certain benchmarks is a mile long. Or think about paid parental leave, which has been proven to be of massive benefit to a society. Very few companies actually offer it. That's because businesses *aren't* prioritizing the greater good. They somehow see themselves as separate from society, which they aren't.

Here's What to Do

Most businesses have a list of core values and a mission statement. In branding, there's even a general rule that the unspoken end of any mission statement is

"...to make the world a better place." Typically, integrity and being a generally good person are considered "permission to play," meaning you can't be part of a business if you don't have those basic qualities.

To be honest, organizations need to take these statements a bit more literally. As they say, actions speak louder than words. There seems to be a belief that the greater good will happen in some abstract, distant way. Or that any form of doing good is enough, which is why many businesses will point to claims that they're making something cheaper or better. That isn't untrue, but it's an extremely diluted version of serving the greater good. We can do better than that.

Prioritizing the greater good is a mindset shift. It means being more critical of current practices and making hard choices. Making clothing cheaper so that people can afford comfortable, clean clothing is admirable. But if that clothing is made in unfair labor conditions (spoiler: it is), then the ultimate greater good is not being served.

If you're in a position to do so, make sure that your organization's methods of "doing good" are significant and concrete (think: TOMS donating a pair of shoes for every pair sold). If not, pick something specific that is in your purview. That could mean fighting for fair pay, representation, or upward mobility—anything you can directly influence that moves the needle.

It really does come back to choosing one thing over another. If there is a choice to do something that is more beneficial for the world, make that choice. Yes, it means something else will be changed or sacrificed—that's the point.

Take Action

The world is changing. Companies have to accept responsibility for the consequences of their actions. No matter what position you are in, you can bring awareness to this concept. Suggest changes, switch processes, add new programs. Make the greater good a *real* priority.

100. Value People over Profits

Help People Feel: *Valued*

Harmful Habit: *Greed and Exploitation*

Successful Strategy: *A Healthy, Happy Life for All*

What's Gone Wrong

This final topic should come as no surprise: Value people over profits. If your company lives by this rule, you have the best possible chance for creating a positive workplace with a healthy culture and happy people.

Unfortunately, businesses have been prioritizing profits forever. Most people will tell you that profit is the reason for businesses to exist. But in our current late-stage capitalism world, as it's sometimes called, there's more to it. Yes, businesses exist for profit. They are also major sociological entities with responsibilities to those societies. Further, consumers are fed up with greed and lack of conscience. Businesses that continue to operate the old way are already struggling to compete.

The public *cares* about the topics in this book, even if lots of organizations and people in power don't. They don't want to work for *or buy from* corporations that exploit and abuse people; that makes the world worse instead of making it better. Smart and caring consumers will see right through corporate doublespeak—so it's time to get your company on the right side of the line.

Here's What to Do

Even though valuing people over profit sounds like an idealistic goal, it's actually pretty simple to execute. Just wake up every day and do the right thing, even if it isn't the way it's always been done. If you want to break it down a bit more, then you can split your efforts into proactive and reactive actions.

Proactive Actions

There are probably some things that you know, right now, could be better. Take initiative in whatever manner you are able and do something about it. If you need to hire more people, ask for the budget. If you need to discipline an employee whose disrespectful behavior has been ignored, make it happen. You could even go revisit the table of contents in this book and pick a few areas you want to fix.

Reactive Actions

Some things are going to come up that you aren't thinking of right now (or possibly that you aren't even currently aware of). When you encounter those moments, you will have a choice to make. You can either automatically react the way you used to, or you can take more time for self-reflection and really consider your choices. It will take some work, but commit yourself to fighting for people. It will be the most rewarding and powerful choice you ever make in your career.

Remember, you're not alone in all of this. Yes, it may feel lonely and defeating sometimes. But this is a growing movement that can't be stopped. You are probably surrounded by people who know what really matters in this world. They just aren't usually the ones with power...yet.

Take Action

If you make one change after reading this book, make it the choice to value people over profit. Businesses don't have to be soulless machines that exploit everything and everyone. They—and you—can be a force for good. Profits shouldn't come at the detriment of physical and mental health, nor should they be the enemy of happiness. You get to choose how you make money for yourself and your business. Don't do it at people's expense.

Conclusion: Every Little Change Matters

The world is changing. So are people's expectations for themselves and their lives—including their work lives. People are no longer willing to accept that "work sucks, so get over it." And they shouldn't have to!

The workplace is changing too—it must. It needs to be more equitable, more employee-centered, and more supportive. That isn't a fad that's going away; it's what workers and consumers are demanding. Workers essentially all want the same thing: They want to feel safe, respected, and valued. While you can't *make* people feel anything, you can create healthy, realistic conditions that give people a chance to feel those things. A chance to feel happy at work.

If you've learned one thing from this book, hopefully it's that positive workplace culture isn't a buzzword. It's a choice to prioritize people over profits. To be less of a controlling boss and more of a caring leader. That's a major philosophical and operational divergence from the past.

It's important to acknowledge that you are just one person, and even if you are very influential in your organization, you're still part of a system. You're likely to encounter some resistance from people who don't want to let go of "the way we've always done it." But every change you lead pulls everyone in the right direction. You can build a positive workplace culture one small step at a time.

For each change that you make, remember that you impact everyone around you. While the big, systemic overhauls are rewarding, so are the small, but meaningful, individual changes. So, even if you feel like you aren't making as big of an impact as you want, don't forget that you're helping your team members live healthier, richer lives. They deserve that. And you do too.

So, be real. Be true. And be happy...~~at work~~ everywhere.

Additional Resources

Books

Naked at Work: A Leader's Guide to Fearless Authenticity by Danessa Knaupp

Radical Candor: Be a Kick-Ass Boss Without Losing Your Humanity by Kim Scott

The Power of Moments: Why Certain Experiences Have Extraordinary Impact by Chip Heath and Dan Heath

Atomic Habits: An Easy & Proven Way to Build Good Habits & Break Bad Ones by James Clear

Turn the Ship Around!: A True Story of Turning Followers Into Leaders by L. David Marquet with foreword by Stephen R. Covey

Workquake: Embracing the Aftershocks of COVID-19 to Create a Better Model of Working by Steve Cadigan

Quiet: The Power of Introverts in a World That Can't Stop Talking by Susan Cain

Why Do So Many Incompetent Men Become Leaders? (And How to Fix It) by Tomas Chamorro-Premuzic

The Pink Elephant: A Practical Guide to Creating an Anti-Racist Organization by Janice Gassam Asare, PhD

Podcasts

Pop! On Leadership with Virginia Martinez and Kara Kirby

Brave and Purposeful Leadership with Alexandra Young

People Problems with Alexa Baggio and Tyson Mackenzie

Work Appropriate with Anne Helen Petersen

Culture Happens from the HubSpot Podcast Network

reWorked: The Workplace Inclusion Podcast from EW Group

Social Media Accounts

@clarabellecwb on TikTok, who is flipping the script on microaggressions and racial inequity

@hrsagentofchaos on TikTok, who is telling the real truth about HR and the corporate world

@brilliantlead on TikTok or www.thebrilliantlead.com

@coachnaveed on TikTok and LinkedIn

@danfromhr on TikTok, LinkedIn, or www.danfromhr.com

@hrmanifesto on TikTok, YouTube, Instagram, or www.thehrmanifesto.com

@newageceo on TikTok

@randallupshawlearning on TikTok or www.randallupshawlearning.com

@_thehrqueen on TikTok or www.thehrqueen.com

You can also keep up with Robyn on TikTok at @courageousleadership or at RobynLGarrett.com.

Index